SUBMARINE

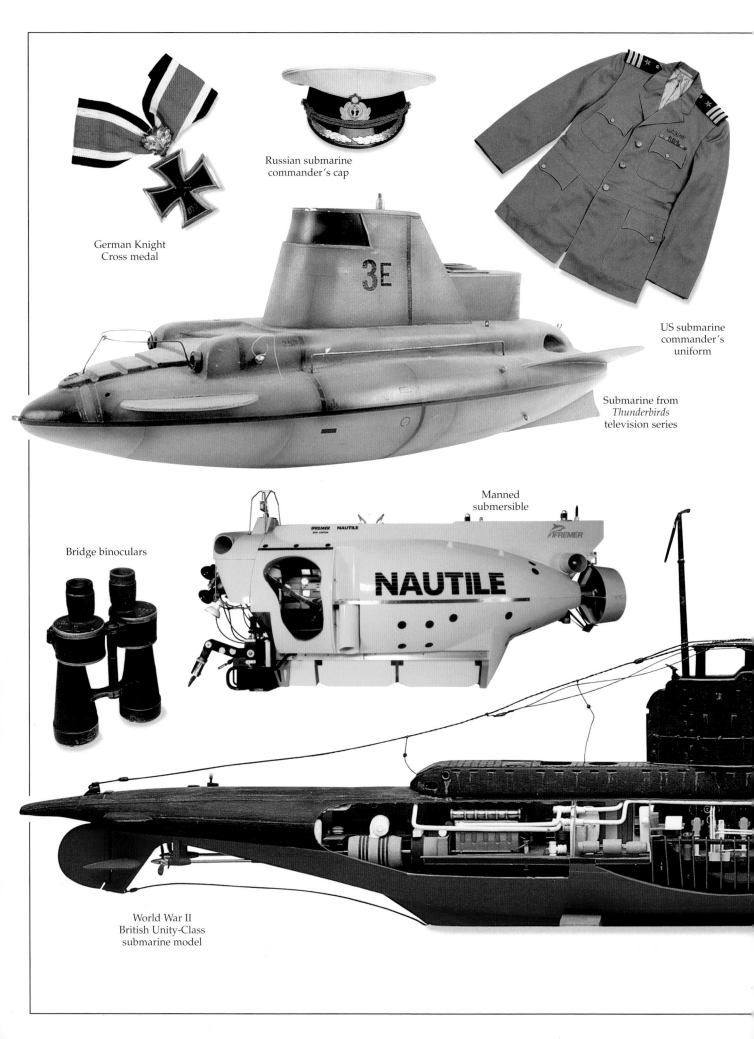

German Knight
Cross medal

Russian submarine
commander's cap

US submarine
commander's
uniform

Submarine from
Thunderbirds
television series

Manned
submersible

Bridge binoculars

NAUTILE

World War II
British Unity-Class
submarine model

US submarine
shoulder patch

US submarine
shoulder patch

SUBMARINE

Written by
NEIL MALLARD

In association with
THE U.S. NAVY SUBMARINE FORCE MUSEUM

German U-boat
pressure gauge

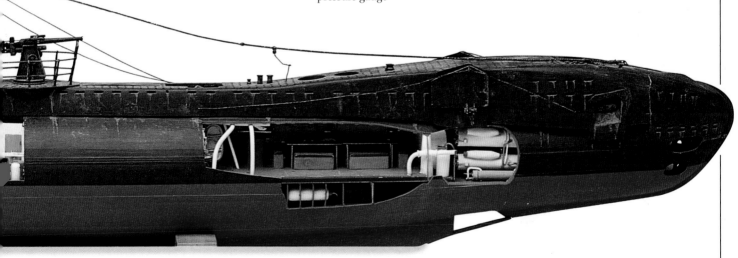

Model of
Garrett's *Resurgam*

Soviet Navy
submarine pennant

Model of Russian
Oscar-Class
submarine

Model of World War I
British Unity-Class
submarine

DK

LONDON, NEW YORK,
MELBOURNE, MUNICH, AND DELHI

Editor Andrea Mills
Designers Tim Brown, Ann Cannings
Project editor Giles Sparrow
Senior editor Kitty Blount
Managing editor Linda Esposito
Managing art editor Jane Thomas
Digital artwork Robin Hunter
Production controller Erica Rosen
Special photography Andy Crawford, Steve Tanner
Picture researchers Sean Hunter, Harriet Mills
Picture librarians Sarah Mills, Karl Stange, Gemma Woodward
DTP designer Siu Yin Ho
Jacket designer Chris Drew

Consultant
Commander J.J.Tall, OBE RN
Director of the Royal Navy Submarine Museum

This Eyewitness ® Guide has been conceived by
Dorling Kindersley Limited and Editions Gallimard

First American Edition, 2003
Published in the United States by
DK Publishing, Inc.
375 Hudson Street
New York, New York 10014

03 04 05 06 07 08 10 9 8 7 6 5 4 3 2 1

Copyright © 2003 Dorling Kindersley Limited

A Cataloging-in-Publication record for this book
is available from the Library of Congress.

ISBN 0-7894-9501-5

Color reproduction by Colourscan, Singapore

Printed in China by Toppan Printing Co., (Shenzhen) Ltd.

German Enigma
coding machine

US submarine
shoulder patch

German submarine
escape breathing
apparatus

Discover more at

www.dk.com

Contents

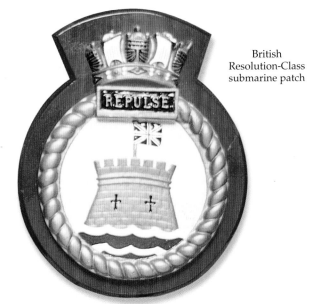

British Resolution-Class submarine patch

What is a submarine?

A SUBMARINE IS AN underwater craft whose invention revolutionized war at sea and which has enabled humans to explore the hidden world beneath the ocean surface. Submarines range in size from a small car to giant vessels twice the size of a jumbo jet. Their shape, method of propulsion, and function also vary widely. Submersibles are designed to undertake short journeys, while nuclear-powered subs can travel around the world without stopping. Specialized vessels can go to great depths to conduct research. They are lowered by a wire from a mother ship. Submarines are also used for fun. These pleasure submarines allow tourists to view underwater life.

U-BOAT
In both world wars, the U-boat was one of Germany's most feared weapons. Ranging far and wide throughout the world's shipping lanes, U-boats gave Germany its best hope of starving out the British through sinking the merchant ships carrying their supplies. Eventually, the U-boats were beaten by the convoy system and the combined forces of aircraft and surface warships.

SUBMARINE "EYES"
The periscope allows a submarine to peek at the outside world with little chance of being seen itself. Most submarines have two periscopes, one with a wide angle for searching an expanse of open ocean and the other a thin tube for attacking at close range. With a flick of a handle, the submarine captain can magnify a target up to six times, making it easier to identify and attack.

SUBMARINE ATTACK
During the two world wars, millions of tons of shipping fell victim to the submarines of both sides. Submarines were able to use their cloak of invisibility unchallenged for many years, until technology provided the hunters with radar in aircraft and ASDIC (sonar) in ships. This sequence of photographs taken through a submarine periscope in World War II shows a destroyer sinking after taking a direct hit from a torpedo.

In 1915, a shot fired by a Turkish gunboat managed to hit this periscope belonging to a British submarine.

"It is possible to make a shippe or boate that may goe under the water to the bottom, and so come up again at your pleasure."

WILLIAM BOURNE
1578

NUCLEAR SUBMARINE

The introduction of nuclear power into submarines led to another revolution in naval warfare. Unlike the relatively slow diesel-electric submarines, nuclear-powered subs could travel faster than their selected targets. In addition, because a nuclear reactor does not need oxygen, the submarines rarely had to visit the surface and could stay on patrol for months rather than weeks. Due to their unlimited power, nuclear-powered submarines could also be built large enough to carry huge intercontinental ballistic missiles.

SUBMERSIBLE

Today, submersibles are used for a wide variety of tasks, from underwater search-and-rescue missions to surveying the seabed and repairing oil rigs or telecommunication cables. Built in Finland and operated by Russian scientists, *Mir I* (pictured above) and *Mir II* were launched in 1987. They are among a number of submersibles capable of diving to more than 20,000 ft (6,100 m).

US Navy diver descending to enter the submarine

TOURIST SUB

The first tourist submarine emerged from a craft designed by Frenchman Claude Goubet in 1899 (p. 16), which was eventually sold to a Swiss businessman and used for voyages under Lake Geneva. Submarine tourism took off after World War II, with the construction of a wide range of craft with capacities of up to 64 people. These operate mainly in the Caribbean and off the coast of Florida.

The clear waters of the Caribbean provide a great view for tourists

Nuclear submarine USS Woodrow Wilson on underwater entry and exit exercises

LIFE ON BOARD

Submariners do not expect to enjoy the luxuries of a surface ship, such as being able to move around freely and breathe fresh air. Comradeship helps to make up for living in cramped conditions. Here, crewmen on a nuclear submarine enjoy a game of cards. Once it was impossible even to wash, let alone shower, and food came mainly from cans. Conditions are much more comfortable today, although teamwork is still vital.

How a submarine works

IN THE SAME WAY that an iceberg is mostly hidden underwater, there is much more to a submarine than is visible on the surface. The narrow deck rests on top of a rounded hull that bulges outward and is divided into an inner and outer section. Between the sections are ballast tanks that are filled with seawater to submerge the submarine, then blown dry with compressed air to bring the boat back to the surface. The physics of "ballasting" was first suggested in 1578 by an English gunner, William Bourne, and the process was perfected in the late 19th century. An engine drives one or more propellers at the stern (rear) to push the submarine through the water (pp. 10–11), the rudder allows it to steer, and winglike hydroplanes keep the submarine level or change its depth.

One of two propellers

After hydroplanes for depth control

Conning tower and mast

Ballast tanks attached to hull

Vent for ballast tanks

Forward hydroplanes

A CLASSIC SUBMARINE
The British D-Class, launched in 1908–11, was a major step forward in submarine design. Larger than previous models, these 600-ton submarines were also among the first to use diesel engines. They had saddle tanks for ballast and a top surface speed of 14 knots.

Ventilation intake

Casing for crew to walk on

BALLAST TANKS
Objects float or sink in water according to how dense they are. Filling ballast tanks with water enables a submarine to increase its density. To dive, the air is allowed to escape through vents, and the ballast tanks fill with water. The sub sinks until it "hovers" underwater, and maintains this neutral buoyancy through the use of internal trim tanks. To surface again, high-pressure air forces the water out.

1. Submarine with ballast tanks full of air

2. Vents open and water enters tanks, forcing out the air.

3. Submarine sinks until it "floats" underwater.

4. Air is blown into tanks to force out the water.

5. Submarine rises.

6. Fully buoyant submarine reaches the surface.

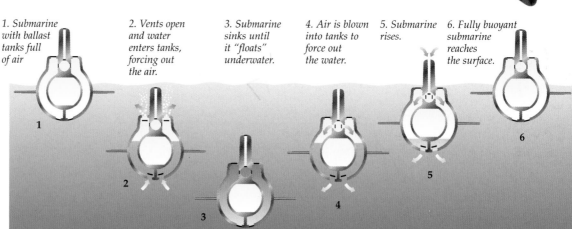

MANEUVERABILITY
Modern nuclear submarines are capable of rapid maneuvers that would tear apart a more traditional submarine. This photograph shows a USN Los Angeles-Class submarine performing an emergency surfacing exercise. The submarine blows its ballast tanks with high-pressure air, tilts its hydroplanes to point it sharply upward, and propels at maximum speed. The submarine has to take care not to leap right out of the water!

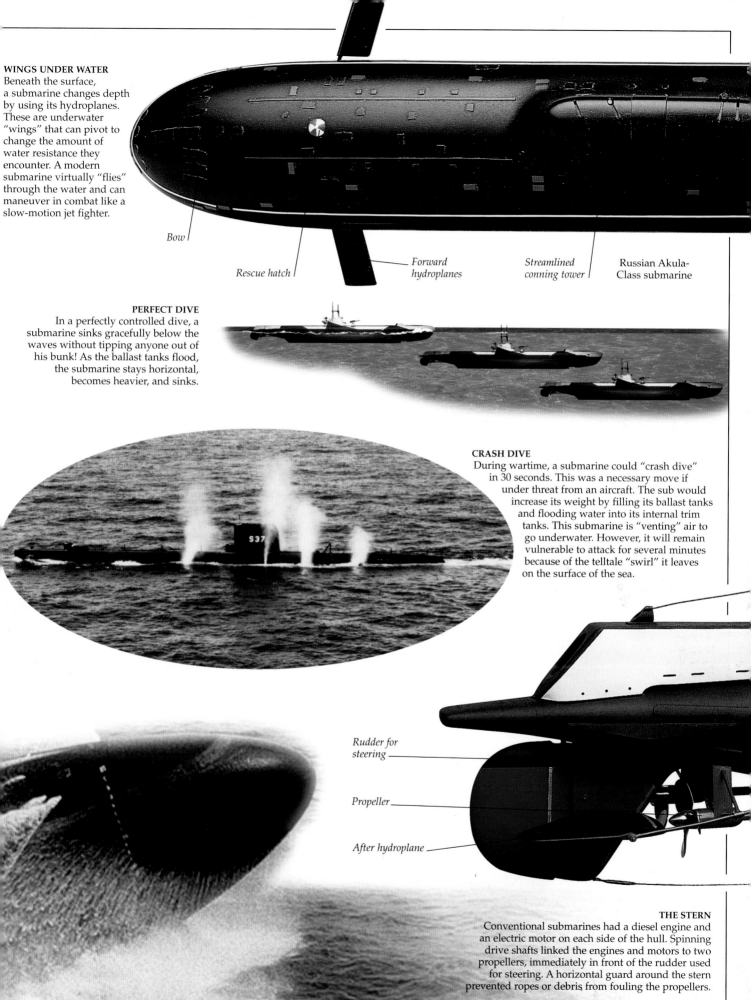

WINGS UNDER WATER
Beneath the surface, a submarine changes depth by using its hydroplanes. These are underwater "wings" that can pivot to change the amount of water resistance they encounter. A modern submarine virtually "flies" through the water and can maneuver in combat like a slow-motion jet fighter.

Bow

Rescue hatch

Forward hydroplanes

Streamlined conning tower

Russian Akula-Class submarine

PERFECT DIVE
In a perfectly controlled dive, a submarine sinks gracefully below the waves without tipping anyone out of his bunk! As the ballast tanks flood, the submarine stays horizontal, becomes heavier, and sinks.

CRASH DIVE
During wartime, a submarine could "crash dive" in 30 seconds. This was a necessary move if under threat from an aircraft. The sub would increase its weight by filling its ballast tanks and flooding water into its internal trim tanks. This submarine is "venting" air to go underwater. However, it will remain vulnerable to attack for several minutes because of the telltale "swirl" it leaves on the surface of the sea.

Rudder for steering

Propeller

After hydroplane

THE STERN
Conventional submarines had a diesel engine and an electric motor on each side of the hull. Spinning drive shafts linked the engines and motors to two propellers, immediately in front of the rudder used for steering. A horizontal guard around the stern prevented ropes or debris from fouling the propellers.

Submarine propulsion

For thousands of years, ships of all sizes had been driven by the wind or by paddles. Wind power was an impossibility for submarines, and so at first the only option was to use oars. During the 1700s, the invention of the screw propeller allowed progress to be made in submarine design, but it still relied on human muscle power. Mechanisms such as clockwork, steam engines, and electrical motors all emerged during the 19th century. However, the major breakthrough was the internal combustion engine linked to a battery. Highly volatile gasoline was the only fuel available in the early days, but this gradually gave way to safer fuels such as kerosene and diesel.

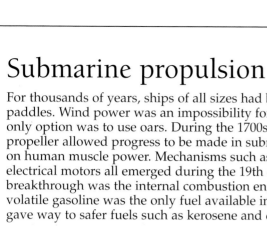

Type XXI
U-boat

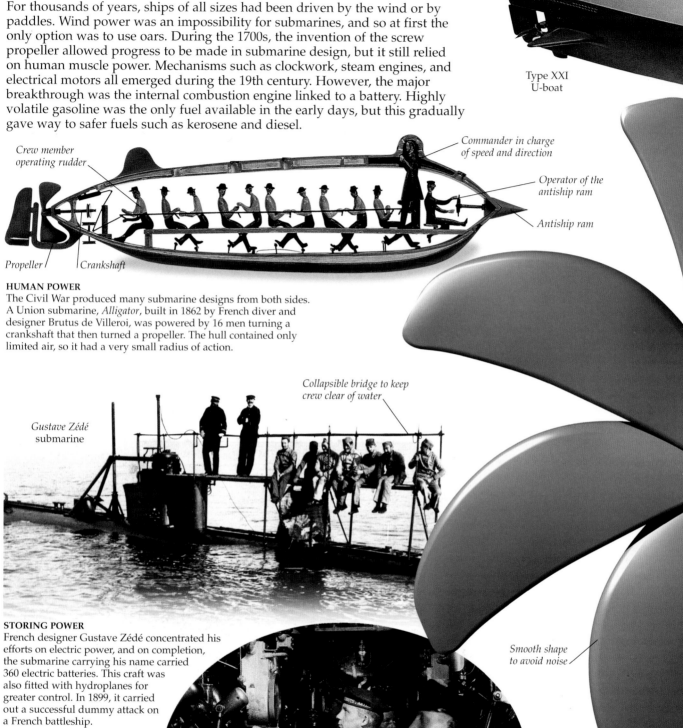

Crew member operating rudder

Commander in charge of speed and direction

Operator of the antiship ram

Antiship ram

Propeller *Crankshaft*

HUMAN POWER
The Civil War produced many submarine designs from both sides. A Union submarine, *Alligator*, built in 1862 by French diver and designer Brutus de Villeroi, was powered by 16 men turning a crankshaft that then turned a propeller. The hull contained only limited air, so it had a very small radius of action.

Collapsible bridge to keep crew clear of water

Gustave Zédé submarine

STORING POWER
French designer Gustave Zédé concentrated his efforts on electric power, and on completion, the submarine carrying his name carried 360 electric batteries. This craft was also fitted with hydroplanes for greater control. In 1899, it carried out a successful dummy attack on a French battleship.

Smooth shape to avoid noise

Inside the engine room of a World War I U-boat

THE ENGINE ROOM
In diesel-electric submarines, the crew had to learn to live with a combination of engine noise when on the surface and the ever-present smell of diesel fuel when submerged. Officers and their men worked in very cramped conditions with minimal facilities during cruises that could last many days.

SILENT RUNNING
The propeller's size and shape have changed over the years. A turning propeller can be heard by the enemy, so modifications have been introduced to make it run more quietly. Boats have used up to three propellers, but today most submarines have one large "prop."

THE DIESEL-ELECTRIC

By World War II, all submarines afloat used diesel-electric propulsion, and the German Type XXI, which appeared in 1944, was the most streamlined design of this type. By coupling the diesel unit to a generator, the submarine could recharge its batteries while on the surface and then switch to electric power when submerged. The Type XXI had a cruising range of 15,000 miles (24,000 km)—enough to enable it to reach Japan.

Streamlined conning tower

More blades for greater acceleration

British Navy hydrogen peroxide boat

WALTHER BOAT

The German "Walther Boat" used hydrogen peroxide to drive a turbine, producing an underwater speed in excess of 20 knots. Fuel consumption proved very high, however, and so the cruise range at top speed was limited to just 80 miles (128 km). The British Navy continued to experiment with this fuel after the war, but later abandoned the project in favor of nuclear power.

Propeller securing nut

Officer and lookout on the bridge

USSN Los Angeles–Class at speed

Propeller blades accelerate water behind them and create thrust

NUCLEAR PROPULSION

Theoretically, nuclear power gives a submarine unlimited range and underwater endurance, so the main limiting factor on the length of time spent at sea is the amount of food that can be carried for the crew. The heat provided by the reactor is used to boil water, and the resultant steam is used to turn a main engine driving through a clutch onto a shaft, at the end of which is a propeller.

Early dreams and designs

THE DESIRE TO EXPLORE the ocean depths was the motivation for early pioneers of the submarine. As with so many scientific advances, these designers knew little of the problems that lay ahead. The most obvious challenge was how to make the craft sink and then rise again. Beyond that were the problems of maintaining an air supply inside the craft, driving it under water when the propeller had not yet been invented, and ensuring that water did not seep in. The squeezing effect of water pressure even at quite shallow depths and the difference in density between fresh and sea water were two further considerations. As more was learned from experiments, the submarine design we know today began to emerge.

ALEXANDER—THE GREAT DIVER
In 342 BC, Alexander the Great decided to look at what lay under the waters of his empire, so he had a glass diving bell constructed. Legend has it that he, a monkey, and a cockerel entered through a hatch that could be fastened by chains. Then they were all lowered by a long rope to the sea floor, where they had a picnic lunch.

BALLAST BASICS
In 1547, Englishman William Bourne worked out the basic principle of all submarines. To make a boat sink, you had to increase its weight by filling ballast tanks with water. To make it surface again, you pumped the water out. Bourne placed a hollow mast above the water to supply fresh air.

Screw-controlled ballast tanks

Bourne's wooden-hulled design

LEONARDO'S EXPERIMENTS
Leonardo da Vinci (1452–1519) designed an early breathing apparatus. It failed because the proposed breathing tube was more than twice as long as the human windpipe, and so the tube would soon have been dangerously full of carbon dioxide. The tube would need to be short enough to empty completely with a single breath.

Hollow tube

Tie-on mouthpiece

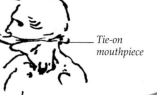

NATURE'S SUBMARINE
"Nautilus" is the most common name for a submarine. It comes from nature's own submarine, *Nautilus popilius*. This sea creature lives within the outer shell of its home. To rise and fall, it pumps out water with gas generated from the inner shells.

BORELLI'S BOAT
In the 1670s, Italian scientist Giovanni Borelli discovered that a fish controls its depth by varying the weight of water carried in its bladder. Using goatskin bladders for ballast tanks, he planned a boat with levers to flood and empty the tanks. He included oars to act like a fish tail and move his boat through the water.

VAN DREBBEL'S ODYSSEY
In 1620, Dutch scientist Cornelius van Drebbel demonstrated to England's King James his oar-driven submersible in a four-mile voyage between Westminster and Greenwich on the Thames River in London. Diaries of the period describe his vessel as an enclosed rowboat with waterproof leather oars. Its hydrodynamic form pulled it underwater when it was propelled ahead by the oarsmen, proving that shape was crucial to submarine design.

FACT OR FICTION?
As the inventors explored the depths, the fiction writers followed. The most successful was 19th-century writer Jules Verne. His *20,000 Leagues under the Sea* (an impossible calculation, since the ocean is not this deep) follows the adventures of a submarine crew. Much of the fiction would later become fact.

WIND UP
During the Anglo-Dutch War of 1652–54, a Frenchman named de Son built a submersible with a clockwork engine for the Dutch. Once it was wound up, it was meant to travel for eight hours, but when the submersible was tested, the paddlewheels failed to go around because of water resistance, and the idea was abandoned.

Propulsion by paddlewheel

Battering ram made this the first underwater warship in history.

Blockade busters

A NAVAL BLOCKADE is established by a group of ships patrolling off a harbor or bay to prevent defending ships from leaving or entering. It is the maritime equivalent of laying siege to a castle and starving the opposition into surrender. This tactic was used on many occasions by the superpowers of the 18th century, the French and British, who had numerous powerful wooden warships. In 1776, during the American Revolution (1775–83), a tiny submersible dared to challenge the might of British blockaders off New York Harbor. It conducted the first submerged attack in history.

Diving propeller for up-and-down movement

Brass cover with six portholes

Reinforced wooden bodywork

Forward movement propeller

Foot pedals to turn the propeller

BUSHNELL'S TURTLE
Designed by American David Bushnell, the *Turtle* required a strong and multitalented operator. The pilot had to navigate, steer, and operate the control pedals with his feet to turn the horizontal propeller. Once close to the target, he had to dive underneath it using the downward propeller. The idea was to screw a limpet mine into the enemy's hull, and then escape before it exploded!

THE TURTLE ATTACKS
In 1776, Sergeant Ezra Lee piloted the *Turtle* underneath the flagship of the British blockading ships, HMS *Eagle*. But he unfortunately tried to screw his mine onto a metal section of the hull. After an exhausting 30 minutes, Lee gave up and fled.

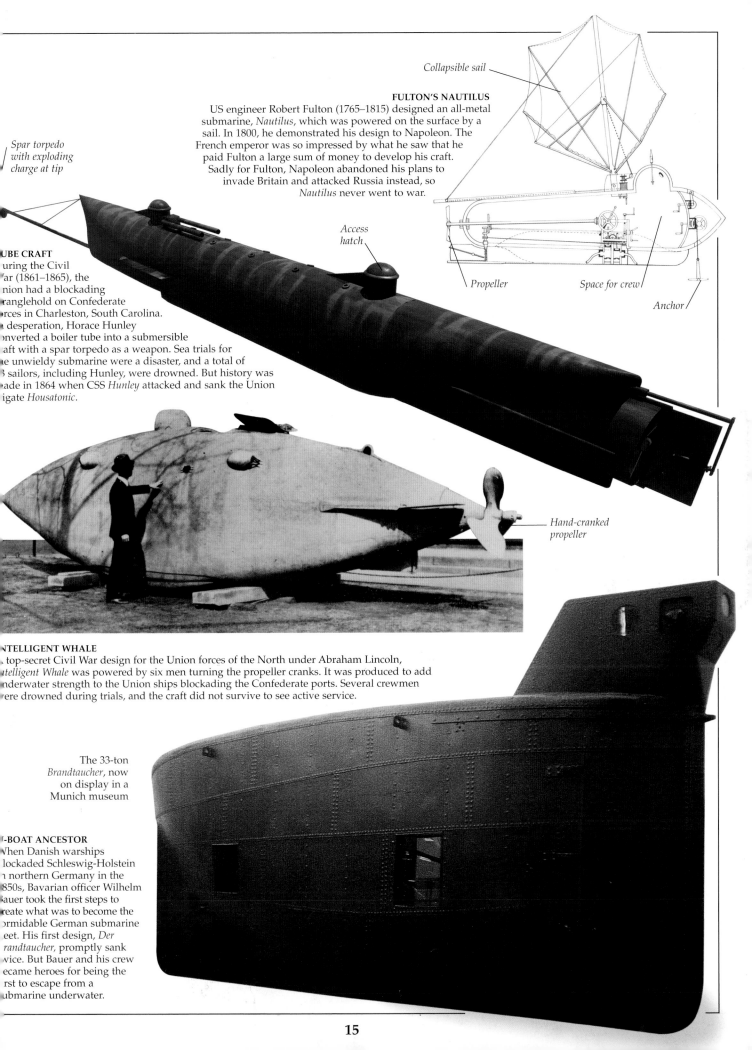

*Spar torpedo
with exploding
charge at tip*

FULTON'S NAUTILUS

Collapsible sail

US engineer Robert Fulton (1765–1815) designed an all-metal submarine, *Nautilus*, which was powered on the surface by a sail. In 1800, he demonstrated his design to Napoleon. The French emperor was so impressed by what he saw that he paid Fulton a large sum of money to develop his craft. Sadly for Fulton, Napoleon abandoned his plans to invade Britain and attacked Russia instead, so *Nautilus* never went to war.

Propeller *Space for crew* *Anchor*

Access hatch

UBE CRAFT

uring the Civil
ar (1861–1865), the
nion had a blockading
ranglehold on Confederate
rces in Charleston, South Carolina.
 desperation, Horace Hunley
onverted a boiler tube into a submersible
aft with a spar torpedo as a weapon. Sea trials for
e unwieldy submarine were a disaster, and a total of
 sailors, including Hunley, were drowned. But history was
ade in 1864 when CSS *Hunley* attacked and sank the Union
igate *Housatonic*.

*Hand-cranked
propeller*

NTELLIGENT WHALE

 top-secret Civil War design for the Union forces of the North under Abraham Lincoln,
telligent Whale was powered by six men turning the propeller cranks. It was produced to add
nderwater strength to the Union ships blockading the Confederate ports. Several crewmen
ere drowned during trials, and the craft did not survive to see active service.

The 33-ton
Brandtaucher, now
on display in a
Munich museum

-BOAT ANCESTOR

Vhen Danish warships
lockaded Schleswig-Holstein
n northern Germany in the
850s, Bavarian officer Wilhelm
auer took the first steps to
reate what was to become the
ormidable German submarine
eet. His first design, *Der
randtaucher*, promptly sank
vice. But Bauer and his crew
ecame heroes for being the
rst to escape from a
ubmarine underwater.

The true submarine is born

By the late 1800s, inventors were working to develop submarines that were practical. None of the earlier designs could be controlled effectively underwater, nor could they be propelled without using human muscle power. The man who finally overcame these problems was Irish-born American John Philip Holland (1841–1914). Around this time, Englishman Robert Whitehead invented the locomotive torpedo, intended at first for use in surface warships. The combination of submarines and torpedoes produced the most lethal development in naval history.

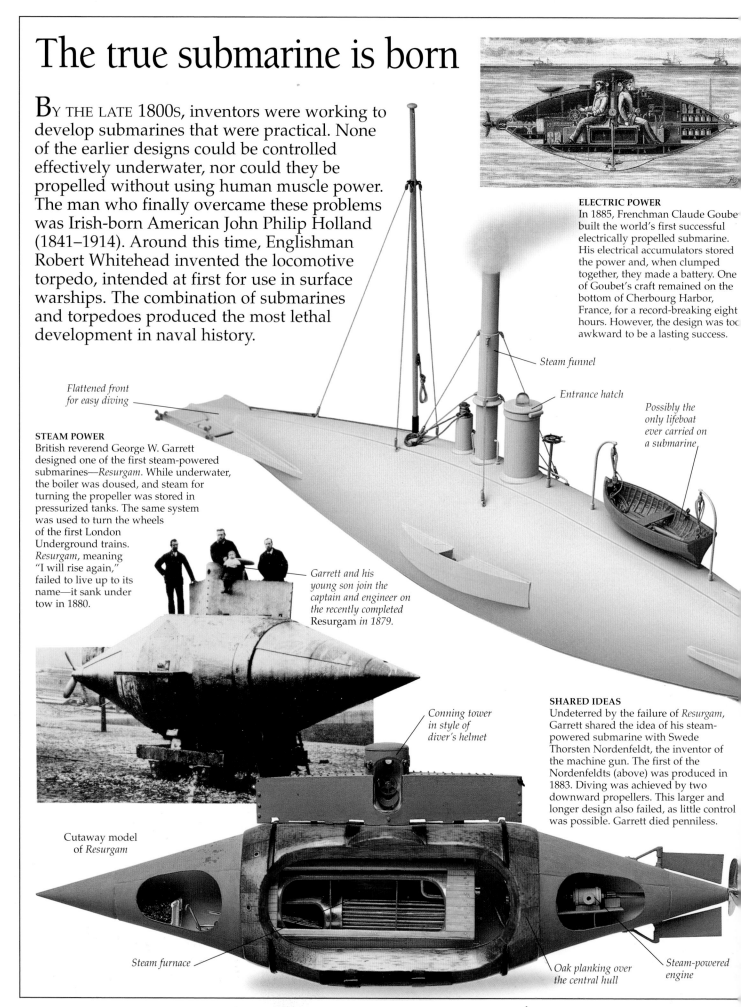

ELECTRIC POWER
In 1885, Frenchman Claude Goube built the world's first successful electrically propelled submarine. His electrical accumulators stored the power and, when clumped together, they made a battery. One of Goubet's craft remained on the bottom of Cherbourg Harbor, France, for a record-breaking eight hours. However, the design was too awkward to be a lasting success.

Steam funnel

Flattened front for easy diving

Entrance hatch

Possibly the only lifeboat ever carried on a submarine

STEAM POWER
British reverend George W. Garrett designed one of the first steam-powered submarines—*Resurgam*. While underwater, the boiler was doused, and steam for turning the propeller was stored in pressurized tanks. The same system was used to turn the wheels of the first London Underground trains. *Resurgam*, meaning "I will rise again," failed to live up to its name—it sank under tow in 1880.

Garrett and his young son join the captain and engineer on the recently completed Resurgam *in 1879.*

Conning tower in style of diver's helmet

SHARED IDEAS
Undeterred by the failure of *Resurgam*, Garrett shared the idea of his steam-powered submarine with Swede Thorsten Nordenfeldt, the inventor of the machine gun. The first of the Nordenfeldts (above) was produced in 1883. Diving was achieved by two downward propellers. This larger and longer design also failed, as little control was possible. Garrett died penniless.

Cutaway model of Resurgam

Steam furnace

Oak planking over the central hull

Steam-powered engine

FIRST SUB
The British Royal Navy's first submarine, *Holland I*, joined the fleet in 1901, and is seen here off Portsmouth, England. The submarine was powered on the surface by a gasoline engine, which operated a generator to charge electric batteries. Once submerged, the engine was stopped and the batteries powered the boat.

JOHN PHILIP HOLLAND
Hailed as the "father of the modern submarine," John Philip Holland is seen here emerging from *Holland VI* in April 1898. He emigrated from Ireland to the United States, where he began his landmark work. His designs were later adopted by the navies of Britain, Japan, Russia, and Sweden.

"The submarine is the coming type of war vessel for sea fighting."

BRITISH ADMIRAL OF THE FLEET, LORD FISHER
May 1913

Explosive charge inside nose cone

Propeller

THE TORPEDO
In 1868, British engineer Robert Whitehead designed and built the first self-propelled torpedo. Powered by compressed air, it was 16 ft (4.8 m) long and carried a 76-lb (34-kg) charge of guncotton to a range of more than 980 ft (300 m). The torpedo, nicknamed the "Devil's Device," was soon used in battle, and for a while it was preferred over the gun as a ship's main armament.

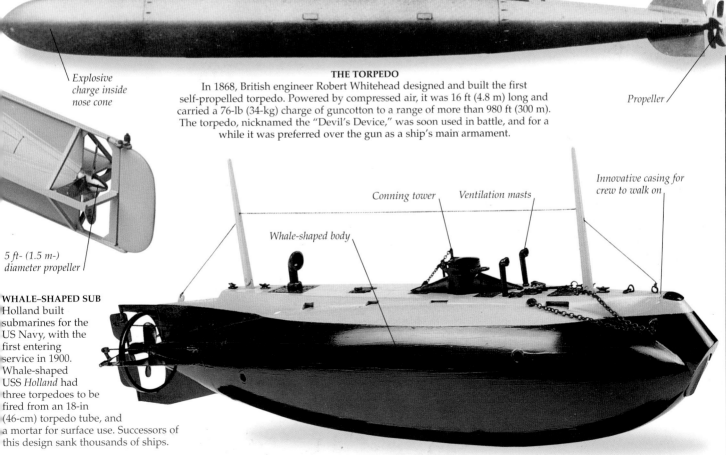

Conning tower   *Ventilation masts*

Innovative casing for crew to walk on

Whale-shaped body

5 ft- (1.5 m-) diameter propeller

WHALE–SHAPED SUB
Holland built submarines for the US Navy, with the first entering service in 1900. Whale-shaped USS *Holland* had three torpedoes to be fired from an 18-in (46-cm) torpedo tube, and a mortar for surface use. Successors of this design sank thousands of ships.

Subs go to war

THE U-BOATS ARE OUT!
In 1914, Germany entered the war with just 20 U-boats. U-boat imagery was widely used for propaganda by the German government to show the destructive capability of the submarine and Germany's military strength.

Woorld War I (1914–18) was the first real submarine war. Germany soon realized that sinking merchant ships bringing food supplies to France and Britain gave them the chance to win a "starvation war." Under international law, submarines had to stop and search a target for prohibited goods before sinking it. But faced with the British blockade, the Germans sank ships without warning. Outraged, the United States joined the war in 1917, and, at last, the convoy system was introduced to enable huge fleets of supply ships to travel in relative safety. Despite earlier success against unarmed ships, the U-boats failed to win the battle.

SHIPPING LOSSES
By the end of the war, German submarines had sunk 5,554 merchant ships. The U-boats also suffered, though. From a total of 372 submarines, they lost 178, most of them sunk by mines. Despite these huge losses, the submarine had proved itself as one of the most decisive weapons of naval power.

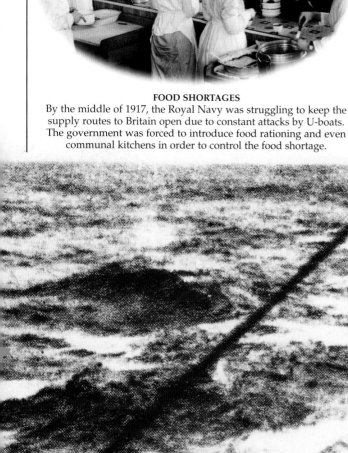

FOOD SHORTAGES
By the middle of 1917, the Royal Navy was struggling to keep the supply routes to Britain open due to constant attacks by U-boats. The government was forced to introduce food rationing and even communal kitchens in order to control the food shortage.

OPEN FIRE
During World War I, there was no method of detecting dived submarines, although a number were caught on the surface and rammed. German U-boats also used cannons on deck to fire at unarmed ships from the surface and so save on torpedoes.

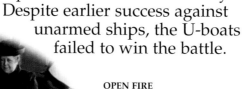

U-boat crew fires a deck cannon to stop an enemy steamer.

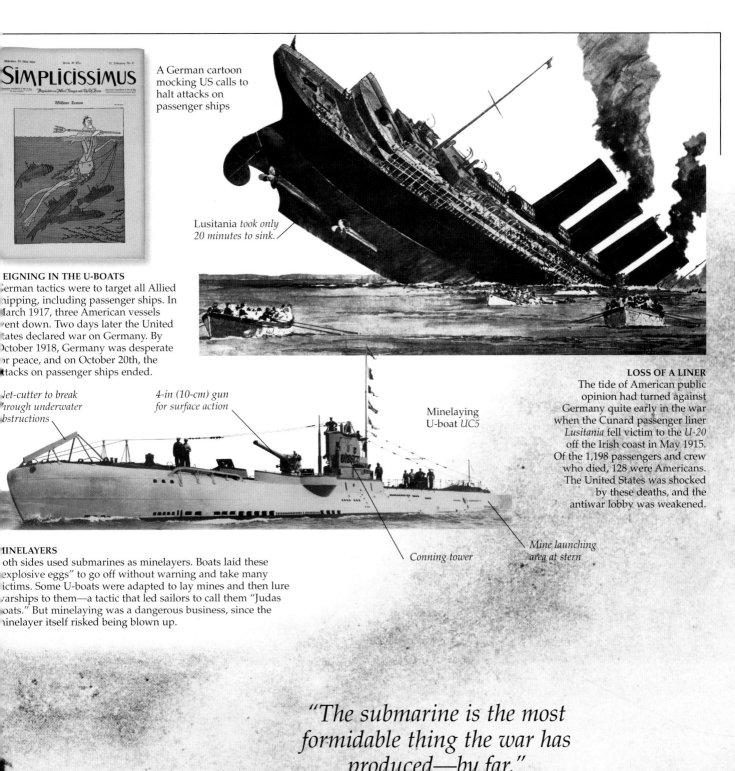

A German cartoon mocking US calls to halt attacks on passenger ships

Lusitania *took only 20 minutes to sink.*

REIGNING IN THE U-BOATS

German tactics were to target all Allied shipping, including passenger ships. In March 1917, three American vessels went down. Two days later the United States declared war on Germany. By October 1918, Germany was desperate for peace, and on October 20th, the attacks on passenger ships ended.

Net-cutter to break through underwater obstructions

4-in (10-cm) gun for surface action

Minelaying U-boat *UC5*

LOSS OF A LINER

The tide of American public opinion had turned against Germany quite early in the war when the Cunard passenger liner *Lusitania* fell victim to the *U-20* off the Irish coast in May 1915. Of the 1,198 passengers and crew who died, 128 were Americans. The United States was shocked by these deaths, and the antiwar lobby was weakened.

Mine launching area at stern

Conning tower

MINELAYERS

Both sides used submarines as minelayers. Boats laid these "explosive eggs" to go off without warning and take many victims. Some U-boats were adapted to lay mines and then lure warships to them—a tactic that led sailors to call them "Judas boats." But minelaying was a dangerous business, since the minelayer itself risked being blown up.

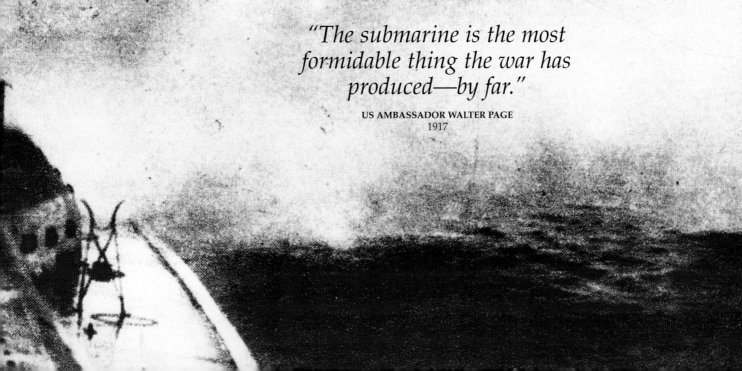

"The submarine is the most formidable thing the war has produced—by far."

US AMBASSADOR WALTER PAGE
1917

Doomed designs

BETWEEN THE WORLD WARS, many new submarines were developed, and most of them failed—often costing lives in the process. These were experimental years, with inventors pushing boundaries to use submarines in different ways. Most were trying to increase the effectiveness and range of submarines. Although many of the designs showed brilliance in tactical thought, the submarines turned out to be disappointing or even disastrous. Submarine designers learned from their mistakes and began to plan a new generation of submarines.

SUBMARINE ON WHEELS
It was easy to recognize a submarine designed by Simon Lake (US; 1866–1945)—it was equipped with wheels. Lake was a great believer in the working qualities of the submarine, so he wanted to make use of the sea floor by allowing his submarines to bump their way along the bottom. Although Lake's designs were always innovative, they never caught on.

K-CLASS
The steam-driven K-Class was introduced into the British Royal Navy in 1916 as a fleet escort and stayed in service until the 1920s. Even though they could reach high speeds, they were extremely clumsy submarines and suffered many mishaps—so many that they became known as the "Kalamitous Ks." *K4* (above) was involved in an accident, as were eight other K-Class submarines.

Communication mast

Four torpedo tubes for attack

Periscope

Elevator for carrying ammunition to gun

Breach for loading shells

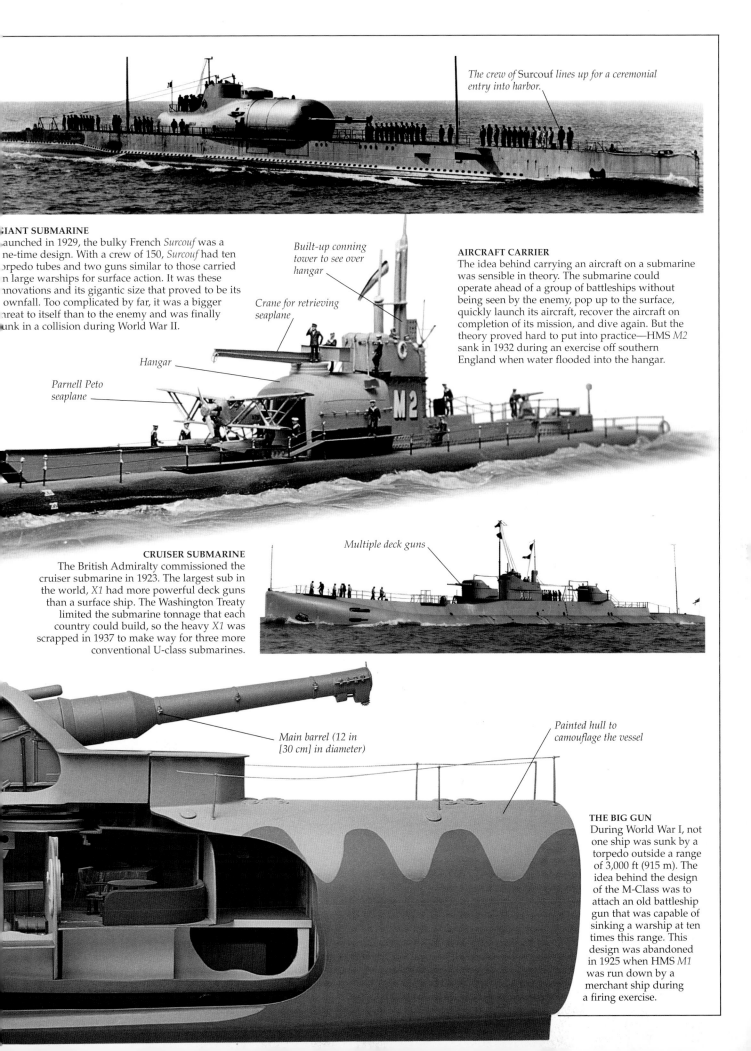

The crew of Surcouf *lines up for a ceremonial entry into harbor.*

GIANT SUBMARINE

Launched in 1929, the bulky French *Surcouf* was a one-time design. With a crew of 150, *Surcouf* had ten torpedo tubes and two guns similar to those carried in large warships for surface action. It was these innovations and its gigantic size that proved to be its downfall. Too complicated by far, it was a bigger threat to itself than to the enemy and was finally sunk in a collision during World War II.

Built-up conning tower to see over hangar

Crane for retrieving seaplane

Hangar

Parnell Peto seaplane

AIRCRAFT CARRIER

The idea behind carrying an aircraft on a submarine was sensible in theory. The submarine could operate ahead of a group of battleships without being seen by the enemy, pop up to the surface, quickly launch its aircraft, recover the aircraft on completion of its mission, and dive again. But the theory proved hard to put into practice—HMS *M2* sank in 1932 during an exercise off southern England when water flooded into the hangar.

CRUISER SUBMARINE

The British Admiralty commissioned the cruiser submarine in 1923. The largest sub in the world, *X1* had more powerful deck guns than a surface ship. The Washington Treaty limited the submarine tonnage that each country could build, so the heavy *X1* was scrapped in 1937 to make way for three more conventional U-class submarines.

Multiple deck guns

Main barrel (12 in [30 cm] in diameter)

Painted hull to camouflage the vessel

THE BIG GUN

During World War I, not one ship was sunk by a torpedo outside a range of 3,000 ft (915 m). The idea behind the design of the M-Class was to attach an old battleship gun that was capable of sinking a warship at ten times this range. This design was abandoned in 1925 when HMS *M1* was run down by a merchant ship during a firing exercise.

World War II

WORLD WAR II (1939–45) brought together the destructive capability of the German U-boats in the Atlantic and of their American equivalents in the Pacific. The result was the loss of millions of tons of merchant shipping, including the almost total destruction of the Japanese merchant fleet. In the Atlantic following major fleet losses in the early years, the war swung against the U-boat. Germany fell behind in the technical race, and there were many more Allied warships and radar-equipped aircraft than U-boats. By 1943, the U-boats became the hunted instead of the hunters. Now called "iron coffins" by crews who would expect to survive no more than three trips, 785 boats were sunk in World War II. Eight out of ten submariners died in action.

GRAND ADMIRAL DONITZ
A U-boat commander in World War I, Karl Donitz went on to mastermind the U-boat campaign in World War II. He started the "wolf pack" system that saw up to 20 submarines attack a single convoy. He briefly succeeded Adolf Hitler in the last weeks of the war.

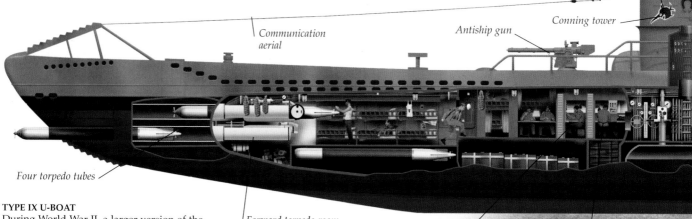

Attack periscope

U-boat emblem

Communication aerial

Antiship gun

Conning tower

Four torpedo tubes

Forward torpedo room and crew's quarters

Hydrophone room

Radio room

TYPE IX U-BOAT
During World War II, a larger version of the Type VII U-boat arrived. The "Nines" acted as attack craft, blockade runners, and "milch cows"—supply ships for wolf packs on extended operations in the Atlantic and Indian oceans.

"The only thing that ever really frightened me during the war was the U-boat peril."
BRITISH PRIME MINISTER WINSTON CHURCHILL

MASS PRODUCTION
The Germans, British, and Americans recognized that large submarine fleets were essential. For Germany, the excellent Type VIIs proved to be the workhorse in the Atlantic; the British S, T, and U classes fought with distinction in the Mediterranean; and the US Gato and Balao classes dominated the Pacific.

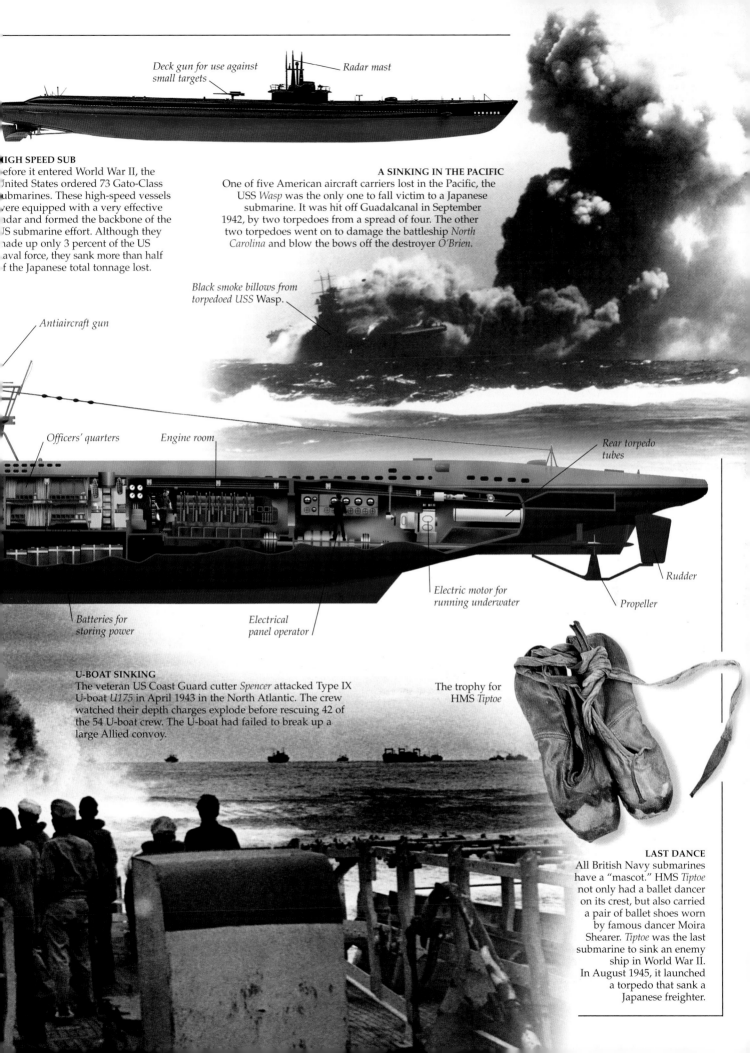

Deck gun for use against small targets

Radar mast

HIGH SPEED SUB

Before it entered World War II, the United States ordered 73 Gato-Class submarines. These high-speed vessels were equipped with a very effective radar and formed the backbone of the US submarine effort. Although they made up only 3 percent of the US naval force, they sank more than half of the Japanese total tonnage lost.

A SINKING IN THE PACIFIC

One of five American aircraft carriers lost in the Pacific, the USS *Wasp* was the only one to fall victim to a Japanese submarine. It was hit off Guadalcanal in September 1942, by two torpedoes from a spread of four. The other two torpedoes went on to damage the battleship *North Carolina* and blow the bows off the destroyer *O'Brien*.

Black smoke billows from torpedoed USS *Wasp*.

Antiaircraft gun

Officers' quarters

Engine room

Rear torpedo tubes

Electric motor for running underwater

Rudder

Propeller

Batteries for storing power

Electrical panel operator

U-BOAT SINKING

The veteran US Coast Guard cutter *Spencer* attacked Type IX U-boat *U175* in April 1943 in the North Atlantic. The crew watched their depth charges explode before rescuing 42 of the 54 U-boat crew. The U-boat had failed to break up a large Allied convoy.

The trophy for HMS *Tiptoe*

LAST DANCE

All British Navy submarines have a "mascot." HMS *Tiptoe* not only had a ballet dancer on its crest, but also carried a pair of ballet shoes worn by famous dancer Moira Shearer. *Tiptoe* was the last submarine to sink an enemy ship in World War II. In August 1945, it launched a torpedo that sank a Japanese freighter.

Mini-submarines

Large submarines could not penetrate well-protected harbors, so they had to extend their capability by other means. The Italians were first to come up with the idea of a "human torpedo"—an electrically propelled craft driven by frogmen that would be carried close to a target by a "mother" submarine. Their range was limited, so the British and the Japanese developed the idea and built mini-submarines with a longer range and a bigger punch. Mini-submarines enjoyed some success during World War II, although it was a one-way mission for many.

Helmet with mask and breathing apparatus

Italian chariot

UNDERWATER CHARIOT
The first use of the human torpedo was during World War I. The Italian Navy resurrected the idea during the 1930s, when a team of engineers converted a standard torpedo into a chariot on which two men rode. The two-man crew dressed as frogmen, and could dive their craft as deep as 30 ft (9 m) to get under defensive nets. It was dangerous and exhausting work. The Italians called their craft *maiale* ("pigs"), the British equivalent was the "chariot."

CHARIOTEER'S HELMET
The crews of the first "chariots" had to make do with gear that was adapted from submarine escape equipment. Later, special equipment like this helmet was developed.

Net cutters

British Mk1 Chariot

THE X-CRAFT
Designed by a World War I submariner, the X-craft was a perfect submarine in miniature. It lacked the range to travel long distances, so it had to be towed to the target area by a "mother" submarine. It was used in a number of operations—cutting subsurface telephone cables in the Far East, landing special forces in France, and leading in the Allied invasion force on D-Day. Its renowned exploits were the crippling of the German battleship *Tirpitz* and the Japanese cruiser *Takao*.

CUTTING THROUGH THE DEFENSES
Antisubmarine nets were used in both world wars to try to stop submarines from getting through or attacking with torpedoes. These nets were hung across harbor entrances or around possible targets. Net cutters were soon developed to hack through them. Here the crew of a British Mk1 Chariot prepares to cut their way through a harbor net.

The only way that the X-craft commander could remain on deck was by strapping himself to a special rail.

X-craft under tow

24

HAWAII FAILURE

As Japanese aircraft swarmed over the US Pacific fleet in Pearl Harbor in December 1941, five *Ko-Hyoteki* submarines moved in to help the attack. The result was a failure—all five were lost, and Kazuo Sakamaki was the only survivor of the ten men involved. He became the first Japanese prisoner of war to be captured by the US.

A German Neger washed up on an Italian beach in 1944

WASHED UP

Germany had little success with mini-submarines, despite producing about 1,000 of various types, including the *Neger, Marder, Molch,* and *Biber*. The survival rate of the *Neger*, which was really a torpedo mounted on a torpedo, was never more than 50 percent.

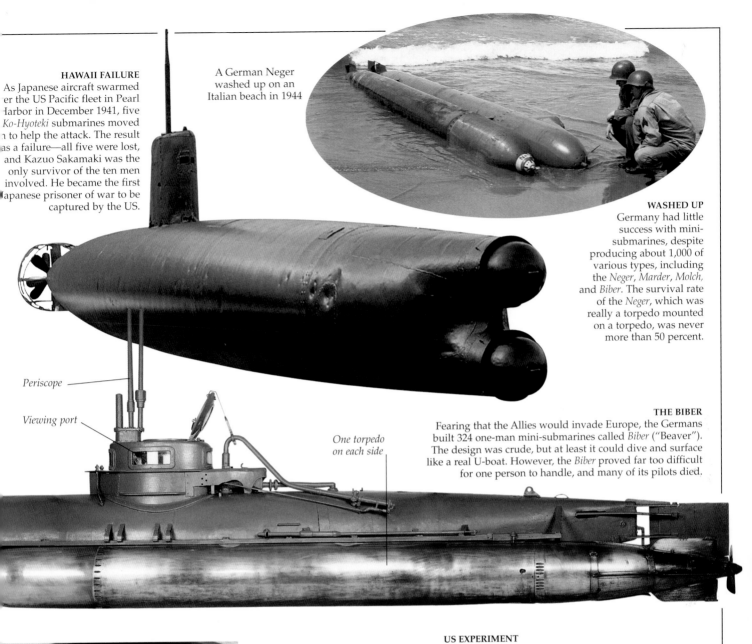

Periscope

Viewing port

One torpedo on each side

THE BIBER

Fearing that the Allies would invade Europe, the Germans built 324 one-man mini-submarines called *Biber* ("Beaver"). The design was crude, but at least it could dive and surface like a real U-boat. However, the *Biber* proved far too difficult for one person to handle, and many of its pilots died.

US EXPERIMENT

Due to the success of the British X-craft during World War II, postwar midgets continued to be developed. North America was surrounded by vast stretches of ocean, so the US Navy had no need for midgets during the war. However, in 1955, the US launched its only experimental midget submarine—SSX1.

Miniature periscope

Draft marks— measurements (in feet) of how much of the submarine is underwater

INSIDE A MINIATURE SUB

Conditions in an X-craft were so uncomfortable that during an operation, two crews were used. The passage crew consisted of three men, and it was their job to keep the craft in perfect condition while under tow. When the target was about 70 miles (110 km) away, the operational crew of four men took over.

The nuclear age

Harnessing nuclear energy for propulsion meant that a submarine no longer had to keep coming to the surface to run its engines and charge its battery, since a nuclear reactor does not need oxygen. Nuclear power provided an unlimited source of heat to turn water into steam, so it allowed the submarine to travel huge distances at very high speed—and even enabled it to travel under the North Pole. In addition, it provided all the electrical power needed to refresh the air for the crew. Now a submarine's endurance was limited only by the amount of food it could carry.

THE OLD RESTRICTIONS
Diesel-electric submarines needed regular supplies of fuel, fresh water, and provisions from submarine depot ships. Also, the battery, which powered the boat while submerged, had to be recharged every day, forcing the ship to surface to access air for engine combustion and crew comfort. This put it at high risk of detection and attack.

NUCLEAR LEGACY
The arrival of the nuclear bomb was a shattering event that marked the end of World War II. But even as the bombs exploded over Nagasaki and Hiroshima, scientists were finding new ways to harness this force—including a more efficient means of powering submarines.

"Nautilus under way on nuclear power."

NAUTILUS COMMANDER WILLIAM ANDERSON
January 17, 1955

NAUTILUS IN NEW YORK
The world's first nuclear-powered submarine was USS *Nautilus*, launched in 1954. Shown here on a flag-waving visit to New York, *Nautilus* traveled submerged for great distances. But it was sister submarine USS *Triton* that in 1960 was the first to travel 36,014 miles (57,947 km) around the world nonstop under the water, taking just 76 days. The first man to circumnavigate the world, Ferdinand Magellan, took three years to complete the same journey in 1519–22.

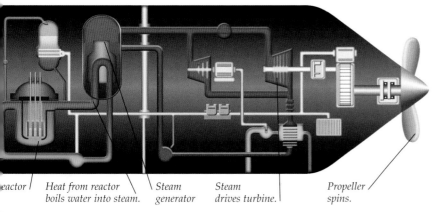

Reactor | Heat from reactor boils water into steam. | Steam generator | Steam drives turbine. | Propeller spins.

STEAM SCIENCE
Using heat from the nuclear reaction, water is turned to steam, which drives a turbine that spins to turn a shaft with a propeller on the end. As the steam cools, it condenses back into water, and the cycle starts again.

UNDER THE ICE
Unhampered by the need to seek fresh air on a daily basis, nuclear submarines could now sail under the polar ice cap. In 1959, USS *Nautilus* passed under the North Pole. Nine days later, USS *Skate* (above) completed the same route, but surfaced through the thin ice on eight occasions, allowing the sailors to sled on the ice and collect icewater as a souvenir.

NUCLEAR SHIPS
Both the US and the Soviet Union tested their nuclear power systems on ships before installing them in submarines. The first US nuclear-powered ship was the freighter *Savannah*. The Soviets placed their nuclear power in the *Lenin*, an icebreaker, which kept open the winter sea lanes to Leningrad (now St. Petersburg).

Lenin breaking the ice

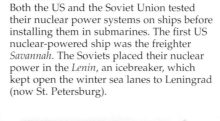

SOVIET DEVELOPMENTS
The Soviet Union's first hunter-killer submarine (SSN) came into service in 1958 (pp. 42–43), and the *Leninsky Komsomol*, commemorated on this stamp, sailed under the North Pole in 1962.

INSIDE A NUCLEAR SUBMARINE
The plentiful supply of electricity, fresh water, fresh air, and three hot meals a day made life onboard USS *Nautilus* quite comfortable for the crew. They enjoyed entertainment such as movies and music to pass the time between on-duty watches.

Balance of power

AFTER WORLD WAR II, the world was divided into two main power blocks—the West (NATO), led by the democratic United States, and the East (Warsaw Pact) led by the communist Soviet Union. The Warsaw Pact could have overrun NATO with its huge numbers of troops and machines, so the West had to stay ahead in weapons technology. The conflict between the East and the West became known as the Cold War, and the technological battle as the arms race. The Cold War was won underwater, as the Soviet Union ran out of money in its bid to match the western submarines. Both fleets are reduced now that the Cold War is over, but they still patrol to deter any would-be nuclear-armed rogue states.

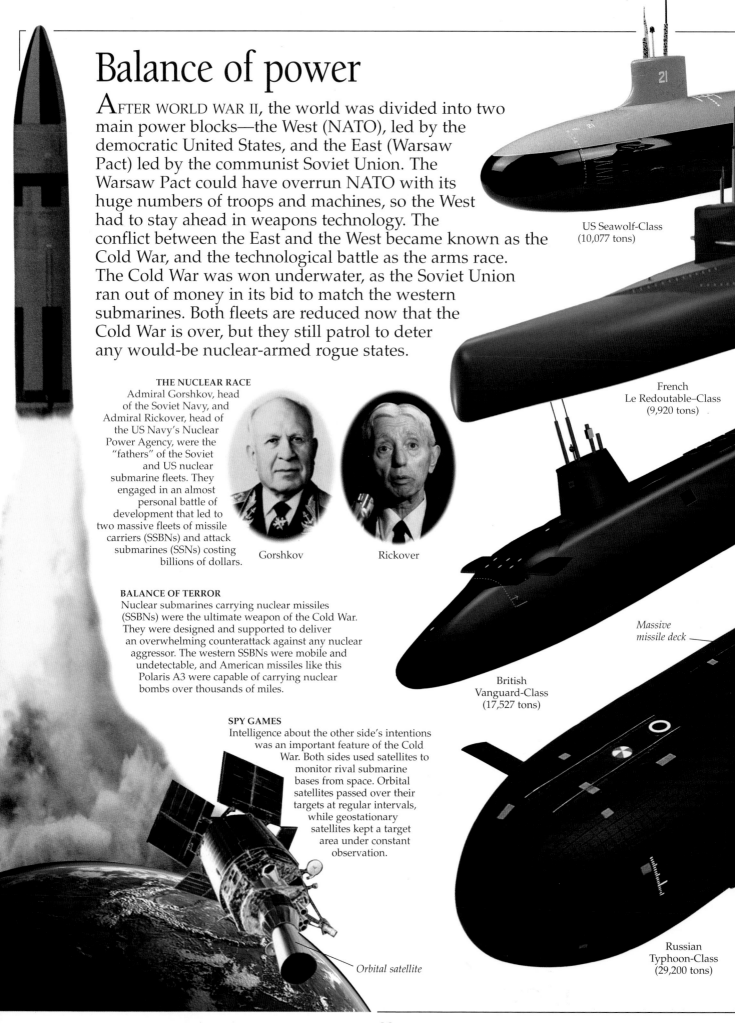

US Seawolf-Class
(10,077 tons)

French
Le Redoutable–Class
(9,920 tons)

THE NUCLEAR RACE
Admiral Gorshkov, head of the Soviet Navy, and Admiral Rickover, head of the US Navy's Nuclear Power Agency, were the "fathers" of the Soviet and US nuclear submarine fleets. They engaged in an almost personal battle of development that led to two massive fleets of missile carriers (SSBNs) and attack submarines (SSNs) costing billions of dollars.

Gorshkov

Rickover

BALANCE OF TERROR
Nuclear submarines carrying nuclear missiles (SSBNs) were the ultimate weapon of the Cold War. They were designed and supported to deliver an overwhelming counterattack against any nuclear aggressor. The western SSBNs were mobile and undetectable, and American missiles like this Polaris A3 were capable of carrying nuclear bombs over thousands of miles.

Massive missile deck

British
Vanguard-Class
(17,527 tons)

SPY GAMES
Intelligence about the other side's intentions was an important feature of the Cold War. Both sides used satellites to monitor rival submarine bases from space. Orbital satellites passed over their targets at regular intervals, while geostationary satellites kept a target area under constant observation.

Orbital satellite

Russian
Typhoon-Class
(29,200 tons)

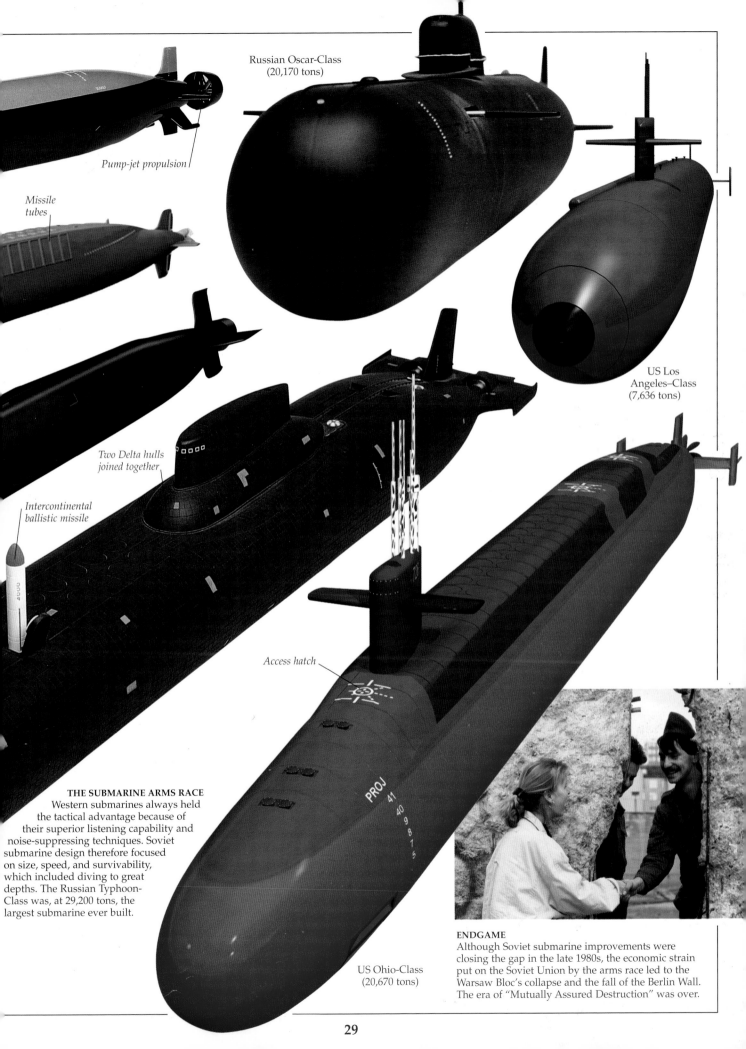

Pump-jet propulsion

Russian Oscar-Class
(20,170 tons)

Missile
tubes

US Los
Angeles–Class
(7,636 tons)

Two Delta hulls
joined together

Intercontinental
ballistic missile

Access hatch

THE SUBMARINE ARMS RACE
Western submarines always held
the tactical advantage because of
their superior listening capability and
noise-suppressing techniques. Soviet
submarine design therefore focused
on size, speed, and survivability,
which included diving to great
depths. The Russian Typhoon-
Class was, at 29,200 tons, the
largest submarine ever built.

US Ohio-Class
(20,670 tons)

ENDGAME
Although Soviet submarine improvements were
closing the gap in the late 1980s, the economic strain
put on the Soviet Union by the arms race led to the
Warsaw Bloc's collapse and the fall of the Berlin Wall.
The era of "Mutually Assured Destruction" was over.

Anatomy of a nuclear submarine

T HE SHIFT FROM CONVENTIONAL to nuclear power in submarines was life-changing for their crews. Gone were the single-deck craft that smelled of diesel oil, throbbed with the sound of the engines, and had stale air. In their place came the hum of ventilation fans, multideck facilities, and reasonable living space. Unlimited electrical power generated by steam turbines was a luxury that saw the introduction of air purification machinery, plentiful drinking water, and even showers. In the West, boats operated on a single nuclear reactor, while those of the Soviet fleet relied on two. Both East and West developed two types of nuclear submarine—comparatively small and fast hunter-killers (SSNs), and enormous missile carriers (SSBNs).

Search and attack periscopes covered with RAM (Radar Absorbent Material)

The size and speed of a modern nuclear submarine require a much taller conning tower than in the past for the sub to remain stable.

BOOMERS

The largest submarines are "Boomers"—the missile carriers that normally go to sea on deterrent patrol for periods of between 60 and 90 days. This British example is a Resolution-Class, introduced in 1967. It carried 16 Polaris missiles as well as six torpedo tubes. Submarines replaced bomber aircraft as the method of delivering nuclear weapons.

Single multibladed propeller

Emergency propulsion motor

Main engine coupled to the propeller shaft

Steam turbo generators for electrical generation

USS SEAWOLF

Originally, 29 boats in the Seawolf Class—the newest and fastest attack US submarine—were to be built. Due to the cost, this has now been scaled down to just three, and they will be succeeded by the more advanced Virginia Class. Seawolf was commissioned in 1997, and can carry up to 50 torpedoes and missiles, or 100 mines. The submarine is very quiet and capable of going on multi-missions.

REACTOR ROOM

The heart of the modern submarine, the nuclear reactor closely monitored at all times. The reactor is normally i the stern half of the submarine, and is started several hours before the boat is scheduled to leave port. If required, it could then remain active for years.

THE ATTACK CENTER

In the past, the captain of a submarine had only his periscope to identify and attack his prey. Today, he has an array of sensors and computers to detect, identify, and work out the attack solution of his target. He may also have a selection of weapons with which to conduct the attack, including the ability to guide his torpedoes directly onto his target.

The inside of a torpedo tube on a Trident submarine

TORPEDOES AWAY!

The days when torpedoes were pulled into position by crews with ropes are over. Now, a 3,000-lb (1,360-kg) American Mk 48 will be moved on skids controlled by hydraulic systems. This is much safer for the crew, and allows weapons officers to make quick changes between the type of weapons loaded in the torpedo tubes.

"Nest" of masts

Thick bulkheads divide main compartments of submarine.

Staircase joins three decks of missile areas.

Forward crew and mess decks

Six torpedo tubes in the bow

Missile inspection hatch

Missile tube

Attack center

Resolution Class—one of the quietest submarines ever built

Torpedo room

THE DRIVING SEAT

Modern submarines are similar to aircraft, and the crew who "fly" them are called planesmen. Strapped into their seats like airline pilots, their responsibility is to keep the boat straight and level by careful use of the bow and stern hydroplanes. As with a jet fighter, a modern submarine can take on large angles when maneuvering at speed—hence the restraining straps.

Planesmen controlling the angle and depth of a submarine

Flying the flag

I͟N 1914, A BRITISH SUBMARINE commander, Lieutenant Max Horton of HMS *E9*, raised a flag bearing a skull and crossbones when he returned from patrol. He had sunk the German battle cruiser *Hela*, and he flew his homemade ensign in response to an earlier accusation that all submarines were pirates. Horton started a tradition that was adopted by other submarine services, and continues to this day. During World War II, US submarines, as well as flying their colorful battle flags, would also tie a broomstick to a periscope if they had achieved a "clean sweep" and sunk all their targets.

MISSION ACCOMPLISHED
The crew of HMS *United* displays a record of their latest success on return to port after a wartime cruise. The skull and crossbones became a centerpiece of British flags. The egg-timer was special to *United* because it had suffered a sustained depth-charge attack.

Insignia on US Gato-Class USS *Piranha*

German U-boat *U-564*

German U-boat *U-124*

German U-boat *U-124*

PERSONAL INSIGNIA
Submarines always carried individual insignia on their conning towers—usually created by the boat's commander. They became a permanent fixture and would often be handed on when there was a change of command.

Silver Star

Nazi flag represents sinking of German ship.

Congressional Medal of Honor

Naval Crosses

Bronze Star

Red Sun flags for Japanese merchant ships sunk or damaged

Symbol for sinking 7 small ships under 500 tons each

Commando raid on railroad on land

Symbol for bombardment of a target such as a factory

Rising Sun flags for Japanese warships sunk or damaged

SUCCESS OF THE HUNTER
As its battle ensign signifies, USS *Barb* was one of the most successful of the US Gato-Class submarines. Its flag (above) boasts a total of 57 attacks. In addition, several symbols represent the medals awarded to the submarine. US submarines such as *Barb* decimated the Japanese surface fleet, sinking 60 percent of its total tonnage. But like all submarine services during both world wars, they paid a heavy price in submariners' lives for their success.

USS *Ray*

USS *William H. Bates*

US flag

NATIONAL EMBLEMS
On entering and leaving harbor, all submarines take the rare opportunity to hoist their national flag above the conning tower. In some cases, a surface cruise will result in a battered flag that then becomes a prized part of the boat's history, as with these flags of the US and British navies.

British flag

MEMORABILIA
Submarines' individual emblems were also displayed on memorabilia. These cigarette lighters were produced for submarine crews, who became members of old comrade associations after leaving naval service. Even in retirement, submariners remain proud of their achievements.

USS *Hyman G. Rickover*

CREW PATCHES
Pride in your vessel has always played a part in naval life, and these shoulder patches were worn by the entire crew of the respective submarines. In wartime, crews do not carry individual ship identification, since this information could help enemy agents assess overall naval strength at sea.

THE LAUNCH
Celebrations mark the launch of USS *Albany* from the shipyard in Newport News, Virginia, in 1987. All submarines going down the slip have crests similar to this on their noses. Combining a motto and a picture, the crest is unique to a submarine. In harbor, submarines put up their crests for decoration until they are about to sail.

33

Life on board

THE SUBMARINE is a fighting machine, and so the first priority is fitting into the hull all the equipment that allows it to do its job with maximum efficiency. The crew comes second, and they have to squeeze in wherever there is space. In small World War II diesel-driven submarines, this meant sleeping with torpedoes and living cheek to cheek with shipmates. Electrical power from the battery was needed for the propulsion motors, so there was little to spare for cooking and making fresh water. Ditching refuse and refreshing the air could only be achieved once a day, when the submarine surfaced at night. The result was a noisy, cramped, smelly, and dangerous place to live and work.

A SPELL ON DECK
Lookouts were the eyes and ears of a submarine when surfaced. They enjoyed daylight and fresh air but, like this World War I U-boat crew, had to be ready to act at the first sign of danger.

Most boxes were plain, but some had elaborate decoration.

A portrait of the box's owner

Family pictures

Letter from home

Sewing kit

Medal

STAYING IN SHAPE
Activity helps to keep a crew mentally and physically fit. Japanese submariners are seen here exercising on deck while the boat is in harbor. During wartime, such exercise would be impossible. A submarine caught on the surface with this many men on deck would have been an easy target.

SHIP'S CATERING
Submariners shared their living space with sacks of potatoes, boxes of vegetables, and loaves of bread. The galley—the kitchen—was tiny, and there was only one hot meal per day, served when the submarine surfaced at night. Canned food of all kinds—such as sardines, vegetables, butter, and jam—was the staple diet.

Razor

Cigarette lighter

DITTY BOX
In the British Royal Navy, the only private space that most submariners enjoyed was a small wooden box called a "ditty box." Here they would keep letters, photographs, money, luxuries, toiletries, and a "housewife"—a sewing kit for making repairs to their uniforms.

MASCOTS AND CHARMS

Submariners were superstitious and frequently carried good-luck charms, such as dolls like this. Horseshoes were often hung in the living quarters, since they were also thought to bring good luck. The mascots all had the same purpose—to ward off death. The most popular superstition in any submarine was that it was good luck to maintain a routine. Everything was done in the same way and at the same time.

FUN AND GAMES

Crewmen indulged in a variety of games known to children all over the world. The most popular of these was a form of parcheesi nicknamed "uckers." This particular game required a combination of luck and skill, but crewmen were so competitive that to be the uckers champion became a major achievement. Cards and dominoes were also popular, but gambling was banned.

HARED REST

n board, long hours could be ent waiting for action, or mply conserving oxygen if a bmarine was forced to remain nder the surface. In many cases, vo crewmen would alternately are one bed—known as "hot-unking." While one was on duty, e other would rest or sleep until was his turn to go on watch.

UXURIES

uring World War I and II, almost very adult smoked. Submariners were exception, despite the constant battle r fresh air. Government cigarettes came ith encouraging propaganda messages nd were often used to trade for chocolate nd other luxuries. Rum was also traded r favors, exchanged for "sippers" and ulpers" from a crewman's bottle.

Tobacco box

WATER SHORTAGE

This German U-boat crewman is using a makeshift bathtub filled with seawater. Standard facilities were much more basic than this. During World War II, the general allowance was half an inch of water in a washing bowl. The priority was to brush your teeth, then wash your face and socks.

How things have changed

The introduction of nuclear power meant that submarines could stay at sea for months on end, so, although the machine remained the most important consideration on board, care for the crew's morale also became a concern. The multideck nuclear-powered craft offers the biggest luxury of all—space. Add the odor-free air, silence, and even limited privacy, and it's clear that conditions have improved dramatically. The ability to stay clean and fresh, eat well, exercise, and relax in a variety of ways is now a routine part of a modern submariner's life.

EXERCISE
The enormous length of a missile submarine provides an unusual opportunity for daily jogging. The captain of the Trident-missile-armed submarine USS *Alabama* is seen here on a run—12 times around the missile area equals a 1-km jog. Other facilities often included on submarines today are exercise machines, and one class of Russian submarine even has a swimming pool and a sauna.

SLEEPING QUARTERS
Living space on nuclear submarines varies with the type of boat. The sheer size of missile submarines offers greater crew space, while hunter-killers are much more confined, with sailors still sleeping between racks of torpedoes. Crew members on the USS *Alabama*, seen here resting in their bunk beds, have individual reading lights to offset the muted red lighting. In addition, there are fresh-air vents, earphones connected to the onboard entertainment system, and a small curtain for privacy. Even though the passing of day to night goes largely unnoticed, routine is maintained by switching the lights to red to indicate it is night.

WASHING AND SHAVING
Fresh water in a nuclear submarine is produced by boiling sea water in distillers, condensing the steam given off, and storing the water in tanks. The salty residue, known as brine, is then pumped over the side. This process uses a lot of electricity, which is not available from the limited storage battery in conventional submarines. Crews can now shower, and shave regularly, as a submariner is doing here on the USS *Jacksonville*. There is even a laundry.

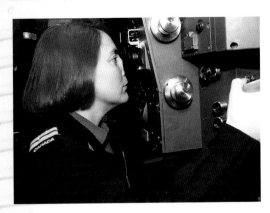

WOMEN ON BOARD

Until recently, most submariners have been male, and even today, wartime crews are likely to be all-male. Less physically demanding peacetime patrols offer wider scope for women to join underwater crews. Canadian Lieutenant Karen O'Connell became the first woman to volunteer for submarine service in 1995 and has been to sea with both the Canadian and Norwegian navies.

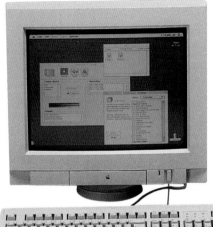

TECHNOLOGY

When off watch, submariners use personal computers for educational purposes and computer games. Other advancements in technology over the years have seen the introduction of VCRs to replace the traditional movie projectors. This allows many more films to be carried on board—submarines often carry about 400 movies, which are exchanged for new releases when the vessel reaches port. Despite the arrival of the Internet and the cell phone, submariners and their families must accept that they will be out of contact with each other for months at a time.

Chef on a Russian submarine

THE GALLEY

Unlike ships, submarines enjoy stability under the surface, and the crew suffers less seasickness. As a result, there is demand for a wider selection of meals. The submarine's cook used to be any member of the crew who showed enthusiasm for the kitchen, and he had to operate from a galley no bigger than a broom cupboard. Today, there are four chefs on each vessel, trained to the highest standards, with excellent cooking facilities. There are even ongoing contests between chefs.

THE MESS

Food for the crew is the only limitation on how long a submarine can be submerged in peacetime. Deep freezers, chillers, cool rooms, and ice-cream machines ensure a supply of quality food, 24 hours a day. Submarines usually go to sea with 90 days of supplies, although extras are carried in case of an extended voyage or an emergency situation. The messes remain the social centers of a submarine, and mealtimes offer an opportunity for crew members to get together and exchange all the latest news about their professional and personal lives.

Up periscope!

THE PERISCOPE IS LIKE AN eye on top of a pole, which, when pushed out of the water, enables the captain of a submerged submarine to see what is happening at the surface. Until recently, the periscope was the primary method both of detecting a target and then of calculating how best to attack with the torpedoes. Today, a submarine's listening devices, such as sonar, are much more important than its "eyes." But when a modern periscope is exposed above the waves, it is not just looking—it also collects electronic data through an integrated aerial, gets a satellite "fix," and receives communication broadcasts from headquarters on land.

USING THE PERISCOPE
Too much use of the periscope could lead to th[e] target taking evasive action or, worse still, th[e] submarine coming under attack. It took grea[t] skill on the part of the submarine captain [to] show only the tip of the periscope abov[e] the surface and absorb critical informatio[n] about the target (such as range an[d] speed) in less than 15 second[s].

TARGET DESTROYED
In wartime, a submarine's standard technique for detecting an enemy ship was through binoculars when the submarine was at the surface. The submarine would follow telltale wisps of smoke on the horizon, and maneuver into an attacking position ahead of the target. It would then dive and use its attack periscope to complete the final stages of the approach, before firing a salvo of torpedoes.

Left grip

High-power lens

Low-power lens

INSIDE A PERISCOPE
This German World War I periscope shows the exterior and interior of a typical U-boat periscope. It provides two different views—low power makes the target 1.5 times larger, while high power makes it 6 times larger.

IDENTIFYING THE TARGET
It was essential for the submarine to know what it was attacking. Warships could counterattack and so usually they were avoided, unless they were a prime target such as an aircraft carrier or a battleship. The submarine's crew would refer to *Jane's Fighting Ships*, the standard illustrated guide to warships and their operational capabilities.

The periscope fits into this weatherproof brass casing.

Periscope trainer models

PERISCOPE TRAINING
Many navies find model ships help when training sailors in how to use the periscope. As a reminder, the most obvious parts of each ship are made bigge[r] on the models. Submariners quickly figure out how to recognize every ship.

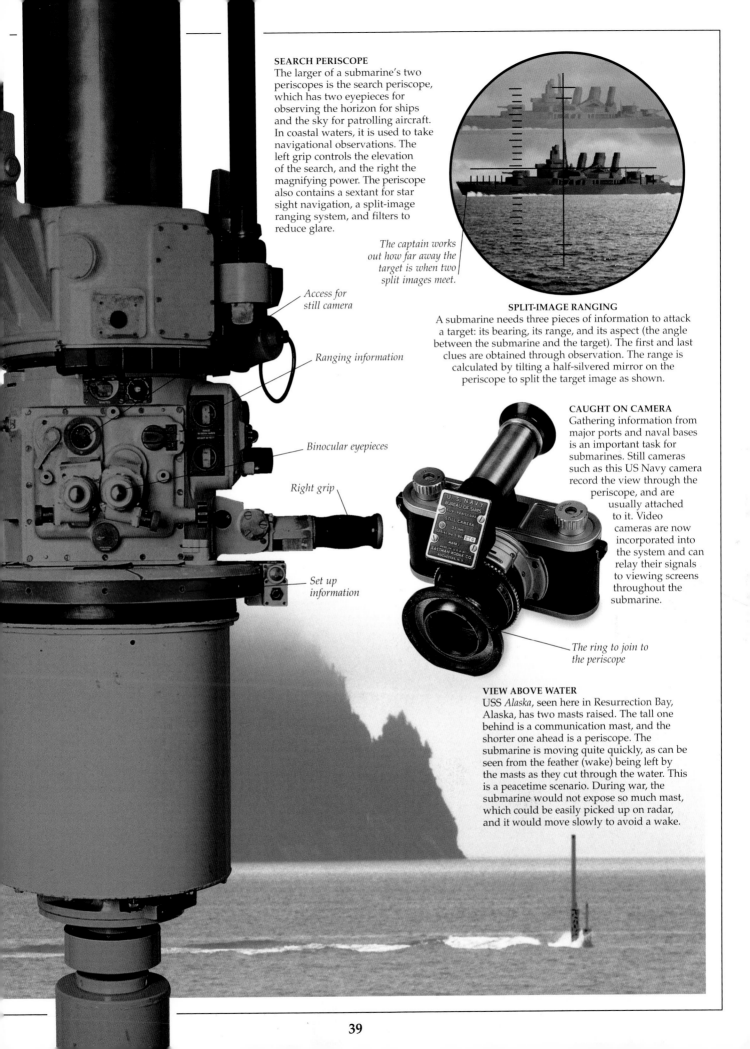

SEARCH PERISCOPE

The larger of a submarine's two periscopes is the search periscope, which has two eyepieces for observing the horizon for ships and the sky for patrolling aircraft. In coastal waters, it is used to take navigational observations. The left grip controls the elevation of the search, and the right the magnifying power. The periscope also contains a sextant for star sight navigation, a split-image ranging system, and filters to reduce glare.

The captain works out how far away the target is when two split images meet.

Access for still camera

Ranging information

Binocular eyepieces

Right grip

Set up information

SPLIT-IMAGE RANGING

A submarine needs three pieces of information to attack a target: its bearing, its range, and its aspect (the angle between the submarine and the target). The first and last clues are obtained through observation. The range is calculated by tilting a half-silvered mirror on the periscope to split the target image as shown.

CAUGHT ON CAMERA

Gathering information from major ports and naval bases is an important task for submarines. Still cameras such as this US Navy camera record the view through the periscope, and are usually attached to it. Video cameras are now incorporated into the system and can relay their signals to viewing screens throughout the submarine.

The ring to join to the periscope

VIEW ABOVE WATER

USS *Alaska*, seen here in Resurrection Bay, Alaska, has two masts raised. The tall one behind is a communication mast, and the shorter one ahead is a periscope. The submarine is moving quite quickly, as can be seen from the feather (wake) being left by the masts as they cut through the water. This is a peacetime scenario. During war, the submarine would not expose so much mast, which could be easily picked up on radar, and it would move slowly to avoid a wake.

Submarine weapons

As a weapon of war, the submarine only realized its full potential when it successfully fired a nuclear missile to hit a land target thousands of miles away. The submarine was no longer limited to war at sea. While maintaining its original role as a torpedo-equipped ship-hunter and intelligence-gatherer, the submarine has expanded its weaponry to include missiles and torpedoes with broader ranges. In the 1990s, the Cold War ended and fleet sizes were reduced. Many US submarines removed their ballistic missiles as the need for deterrent weapons was reduced. Tomahawk cruise missiles replaced them, as tactical capability gained importance.

TARGET CALCULATION
In the early days of submarine warfare, the captain would have to calculate the speed and distance of the target, its size and depth, and the speed at which the torpedo would travel. Calculating the correct time to fire was difficult, because the submarine and target were always moving. This World War II German calculator improved accuracy, although the basic tactic was to fire a "spread" of up to six torpedoes to cover inaccuracies in estimations.

Torpedoes in the bow

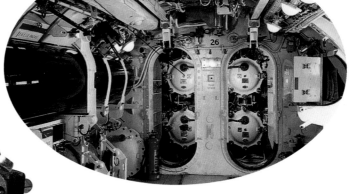

THE TORPEDO ROOM
Small torpedo rooms have given way to huge compartments packed with a variety of weapons. Torpedo tubes were traditionally placed in the bow and stern sections of a submarine. However, many modern submarines have moved the bow tubes and replaced them with modern sonar displays to locate and "hear" their target.

Loading M
48 torpedo
USS *Haddo*

This gyroscope was fitted to German torpedoes in World War II.

TORPEDO ON TRACK
The gyroscope keeps the torpedo traveling in a straight line toward its target. It was first introduced in 1895 by British engineer Robert Whitehead, the inventor of the torpedo. Since then, there have been major changes to the design. Sound-seeking torpedoes now hunt their prey, while wire-guided torpedoes can be steered with great accuracy, even passing information back to their controller.

LOADING RULES
Loading weapons onto a submarine requires accurac
Torpedoes are inserted at a 45° angle to the hull.
Intercontinental missiles, such as Trident, leave
Earth's atmosphere and plunge back onto their targe
so they must be lowered vertically into launch tubes

MISSILE HATCHES
The greater size of the modern submarine has allowed silos of missiles to be mounted outside the hull in vertical tubes. Shown here is a nest of Tomahawk Land Attack missiles in a US Navy Los Angeles–Class SSN. The missiles are blasted from tubes by compressed air, and their rocket motors fire once the sea's surface is cleared. The hatch is then closed and the silo drained of water.

BALLISTIC MISSILES
Ballistic missiles carry nuclear warheads, and Polaris was the first submarine-launched missile of this kind. In a 1960 test flight, it carried a warhead 2,485 miles (4,000 km). By the 1980s, Trident replaced it, with a range of 5,000 miles (8,050 km), a three-stage rocket motor, and 14 nuclear weapons.

CRUISE MISSILE
The Tomahawk Land Attack cruise missile (TLAM) is a low-flying weapon capable of remaining below radar barriers at high subsonic speeds. Launched from vertical tubes inside attack submarines, the missile uses satellite information to ensure that it arrives on target at the exact time required.

MINES
One of the greatest menaces to the submarine is the sea mine, lurking at a wide range of depths, ready to explode and cause huge damage. During the first Gulf War (1990–91), the US Navy lacked antimine facilities, and this led to extensive damage to support ship USS *Tripoli* when it struck an Iraqi mine.

SEA SKIMMER
Fitted to all US Navy and Royal Navy attack submarines, the sub-harpoon can be fired from surface ships and aircraft, too. Armed with a 448-lb (203-kg) high-explosive warhead, it is a radar-controlled sea skimmer with a range of 60 miles (100 km).

Sub-harpoon missile

HMS *Sybil* in World War II

GUNS ON SUBMARINE DECK
In both world wars, submarines tried to conserve their limited number of torpedoes. The alternative was to surface and use deck guns to destroy their targets instead. The gun became an inappropriate weapon as torpedo ranges and accuracy improved. Since then, it has been totally phased out.

> *"Polaris is... to be instantly ready in peacetime to launch missiles in retaliation for a nuclear attack, with the aim of preventing, by its presence and readiness, such a catastrophe from ever occurring. If Polaris ever has to be used, therefore, it has failed."*

VICE-ADMIRAL SIR ARTHUR HEZLET

Antisubmarine warfare

AIRBORNE THREAT
In World War II, submarines spent most of their time on the surface, so aircraft were able to spot and bomb them. The American-built long-range B24 Liberator was a success, closing the "Atlantic gap" created by the limited flying range of previous aircraft. Aircraft were credited with sinking 288 U-boats.

DEPTH-CHARGING
Traditionally, the most effective way to sink a submarine was to use depth charges. These were rolled off the stern of a surface ship. The canister of high explosive inside the charge was set in advance to explode at the estimated depth of the submarine below.

DURING WORLD WAR I, the only way to detect a submarine was with the human eye. Then, the only option was to try ramming it. The depth charge arrived in 1915 and transformed the way a submarine could be attacked. By World War II, electronic "eyes" were invented—sonar sound-seekers beneath the waves, and radar above. These were joined by another powerful weapon in 1944— the antisubmarine homing torpedo. These detection devices and weapons were fitted first into warship escorts, and then into aircraft, which were flown either from shore or from aircraft carriers. The helicopter has recently joined the battle, and completing the antisubmarine team is the most lethal antisubmarine weapon of all—another submarine.

Antitorpedo nets

PROTECTION
Once the threat of the submarine was noted, navies started devising methods of protection. The first of these were nets, placed across narrow channels and around warships. These were backed up by antisubmarine minefields.

Depth charge on its way to a submarine target

SUCCESS RATE
Depth charges destroyed only nine U-boats between 1915 and 1917. As a result, these weapons were further developed, and in 1918, 22 U-boats were sunk. Almost 600 of the 785 U-boats lost during World War II fell to charges. At first they were dropped from the hunting ship, but later they were fired from a distance, giving the submarine little chance of escape.

MODERN ANTISUB WARFARE

Nuclear submarines have the ability to hear, seek, and destroy underwater attackers. This means they are now as important as surface ships for protecting large fleets such as aircraft carrier groups. These modern submarines can easily match, and often beat, the speed and range of surface craft. Together with assistance from aircraft, the submarine has never been more closely watched from the skies, from the surface, or from underwater.

Submarine protecting fleet

Extra-long-range fuel tanks

Surface search radar

MAD boom at the stern

WATCHERS ABOVE
Aircraft such as the RAF Nimrod were specially built to find submarines in the waters below. In the tail of this aircraft is the Magnetic Anomaly Detector (MAD) apparatus, which can detect a large moving metal object underwater.

Searchlight for target identification

HELICOPTER HUNTERS

Most modern frigates and destroyers carry an ASW helicopter. The ability of the helicopter to find and destroy submarines has improved in recent years. It can hop from point to point over the ocean at random, and it is equipped with both active and passive listening devices. It will also carry at least two homing torpedoes for attack.

Seahawk ASW helicopter

Radar dome for surface search

frigates carry uns, missiles, d helicopters

ANTISUBMARINE FRIGATES
Powered by jet engines originally intended for civil and military aircraft, these high-speed ships are capable of covering a lot of ground looking for submarines. As well as searching, their other strength is to attack submarines from farther away by sending their helicopter to where they think the submarine is hiding.

Anti-submarine torpedo

Helicopter drops device into water to listen for submarines

SILENCE IS GOLDEN
Location by sound is now the biggest threat, with aircraft, ships, and hunter-killer submarines listening for their prey. Microphones are even placed on the seabed of known submarine routes to detect any sounds.

ANTISUB SUB
An antisub submarine is the most lethal weapon because it is can go to the same depths as the hunted submarine and seek out its hiding places. Western antisub submarines were quieter and had superior listening devices to their Soviet counterparts until late into the Cold War. Antisub submarines such as the Russian Akula-Class ght) arrived to close the capability gap. The Akula-Class was quieter, more streamlined, and a very efficient earcher. As Akula-Class submarines were rge, they carried lots of listening devices.

Underwater listening device

Communication and navigation

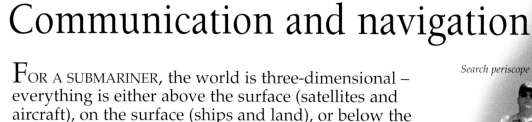

FOR A SUBMARINER, the world is three-dimensional – everything is either above the surface (satellites and aircraft), on the surface (ships and land), or below the surface (changes in temperature and sea-bed trenches). To consider and deal with all of these things, a submarine relies almost entirely on radio waves. But the submarine only listens – transmitting is risky and rare. Information is constantly coming in on screens and charts, sent from satellites and other communications systems. The heart of navigation on a submarine is the Ships Inertial Navigation System (SINS). Used since the 1950s, these sensors adjust to movement, with SINS readouts all over the submarine.

CARRIER PIGEON
Before radio waves transformed communication, the only option for submarines to communicate when out of sight of land was to use carrier pigeons. Pigeons with messages strapped to their legs were launched off the side of the vessel to headquarters.

A German operator decoding from the Enigma machine

ANTENNAE FOREST
Although extending a periscope is one of the most dangerous moves a submarine can make, the equipment for radio and visual sightings must still be available at the top of the conning tower. For the submarine to grab a message ("dump") from a satellite, the communications masts must be raised out of the conning tower, as seen here on this Seawolf submarine.

SECRET CODES
Communicating radio wave messages in secret is essential during wartime. During World War II, the Germans developed the complex Enigma machine that transmitted messages in code. When the Allies captured this decoding machine from a sinking German U-boat, they cracked the code, read the radio traffic, and this helped to win the war at sea.

Antenna to avoid detection

TRAILING ANTENNA
A trailing antenna is used when a submarine wants to listen to routine communications without coming to periscope depth. The Very Low Frequency (VLF) signals take a long time to receive, but there is no risk of detection. The submarine moves slowly, listening to news from home, tactical signals, and intelligence received from shore.

THE SATELLITE

Communication satellites are like big telephone exchanges in the sky. A sub identifies itself with a number to receive messages that have been fed to the satellite by global headquarters. Subs can only transmit and receive information at Super High Frequency (SHF) via a satellite. An attack submarine raises its mast to collect information when it needs to.

Solar panels create satellite transmission power

Satellite aerials or transponders

ECHOSOUNDER

An echosounder is used to find out how far away the seabed is from the submarine. By squirting a short pulse of energy that hits the seabed, an echo is created. The echosounder hears this echo, and the distance is calculated from the time the echo takes to come back. This is even more useful under ice, when submariners set their echosounders to bounce a signal off both the seabed and the ice. These two signals ensure that the submarine moves safely between the two.

Echosounder transmitter and receiver

The pulse of energy is released here

SEXTANT

Navigation by the sun, moon, and stars has been practiced for thousands of years. Before the introduction of electronic navigation aids, when out of sight of land, the geographical position of a submarine was worked out with a sextant. This tool measured the angle of the sun, moon, and stars against the horizon and converted the results into bearing lines. The sextant is still carried on submarines today.

PLOTTING ON MAP

Even the most advanced submarine must use charts to navigate in and out of harbors. Using dividers and a parallel slide on a map, the navigating officer calculates where the submarine is and checks for dangers along the way. Depth of water, wrecks, and rocks are vital information as the officer plots the course. Electronic charts exist today, although a paper chart is carried, too.

Various colors represent the different depths of the contours

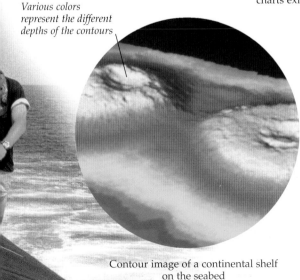

Contour image of a continental shelf on the seabed

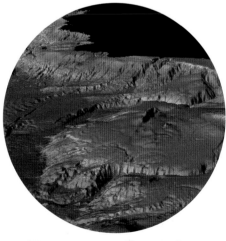

Contour image of the ocean floor off California

BOTTOM CONTOUR NAVIGATION

If a submarine does not want to raise a mast for a satellite "fix," Bottom Contour Navigation is the slower alternative. This is navigation from known contours of the ocean floor. The echosounder helps to draw the shape of what is below the submarine, and parts of the ocean are mapped in such detail that the resulting fix is extremely accurate.

The doomed *Maria*

Submarine disasters

THE FIRST DISASTER
In June 1774, Englishman John Day took a dive in the boat *Maria* and became the first-ever casualty of a submarine disaster. Before he went down, he told people he would go to the bottom of Plymouth Harbor and stay there for 12 hours. Unfortunately, he wrongly calculated the weight of the ballast needed to dive. Neither he nor *Maria* were ever seen again.

Sᴜʙᴍᴀʀɪɴᴇꜱ ᴀʀᴇ ᴅᴀɴɢᴇʀᴏᴜꜱ ᴘʟᴀᴄᴇꜱ to work in. Not only must they resist the ocean, which is squeezing them under great pressure and could quickly sink them in a flood; they also carry high-explosive weapons, oil and air supplies, high-voltage electrical systems, and—in many cases— a nuclear reactor that must be carefully maintained. These dangers are overcome by the skill of their builders, who use the highest-quality materials, and the operation of the crew, who are highly trained to react instantly to a disaster. But accidents do happen.

The conning tower survived the explosion.

Lieutenant Sakuma in full naval uniform

PERSONAL APOLOGY
In April 1910, a Japanese Navy submarine was diving, but it did not shut a valve quickly enough to keep the water out. The boat flooded and sank. Unable to surface, and running out of oxygen, the boat's captain, Lieutenant Sakuma, wrote a personal letter of apology to his Emperor just before he and his crew of 14 died. He finished by asking simply, "Please look after our families."

Sakuma's letter was found by a salvage team.

The bow was cut away by the salvage team.

K-Class submarines accompanying surface fleet

THE BATTLE OF MAY ISLAND
The steam-powered K-Class was the clumsiest design ever produced by the British Navy. Its failure was legendary, most notably in a major exercise in 1918 that became known as the Battle of May Island. By the end of the day, two K-Class submarines had been sunk and several damaged in separate incidents involving collisions. Many British submariners lost their lives.

THE *KURSK* DISASTER

The accident that sank the massive Russian nuclear submarine *Kursk* in August, 2000, was caused first by a torpedo explosion, and was then made much worse by a subsequent fire that caused more explosions. All 118 crewmen died. The shattered hull of *Kursk* was located and raised by a Norwegian salvage team. They returned the wreck to its Arctic base.

Severe damage to the upper deck

The attempt to rescue Thetis

RAISING THE *THETIS*

The greatest peacetime disaster in British Navy history was the loss of HMS *Thetis* through flooding during trials off Liverpool in 1939. A massive effort by the crew to save the craft caused the stern to come completely out of the water. When the oxygen ran out, 99 men died, but four escaped. Salvaged and renamed *Thunderbolt*, the sub was lost in action off Italy in 1943.

SIDON CATASTROPHE

An explosion killed 13 crewmen on the submarine HMS *Sidon* as torpedoes were being loaded on June 16, 1955. Some of the crew was on the bridge at the time, so they escaped unhurt. The accident was caused by high-test peroxide (HTP)—a volatile torpedo fuel. After this disaster, the British Navy stopped using the fuel in its weapons.

Raising the wreck of Sidon

Kursk *was placed in a dry dock for examination.*

A QUESTION OF SALVAGE

Whenever possible, naval authorities try to raise a sunken submarine in order to figure out what caused the disaster. Here, USS *Squalus* is salvaged after sinking in May 1939 with the loss of 26 lives. Despite its association with disaster, *Squalus* was raised and refitted for use throughout World War II.

RESCUE FROM THE DEEP

Two world wars have proved that few crew members survive when a submarine sinks. Peacetime provides a greater chance of helping a boat in trouble. The US, Swedish, and British navies have all built Deep Sea Rescue Vehicles (DSRV), which can assist with getting the crew out of a submarine that has sunk, even at very great depths.

The USN DSRV Mystic *being carried by a "mother" submarine*

Sub safety

Even a small accident at sea in a submarine can turn into a disaster unless it is dealt with immediately and effectively. A flood or fire pose the greatest threat to survival, and so submariners are trained to spot the smallest leak of water and smell the slightest whiff of smoke. Safety devices such as fire extinguishers are scattered throughout the submarine, and if a small fire threatens to spread, then the crew is capable of mustering a full fire brigade between them. Small leaks are prevented from getting bigger by using valves to isolate the risk. Nevertheless these efforts can fail, and research continues into ways to help crew members escape from subs in danger.

DANGEROUS GASES
Early submarines carried miners' lamps and white mice. These mice would give early warning of a build-up of poisonous gases from engine and battery fumes. Mice squeak when they smell carbon monoxide.

Mice are sensitive to gas leaks and fall ill quickly.

AIR RECYCLING
In a flood, the trapped crew need to breathe while they are attempting to escape and during the ascent to the surface. In 1929, Dr. Robert Davis adapted a breathing apparatus he had developed for coal mine disasters into one that could be used in submarine escape. It was small and compact, like an external lung, and was fitted with an oxygen bottle. Named the Davis Submarine Escape Apparatus (DSEA), it was in service in British Royal Navy submarines until the 1950s.

Hall-Rees escape suits

EARLY ESCAPE SYSTEMS
The first ever submarine escape suit was the Hall-Rees equipment designed in 1907. It was a major step forward because it recognized that a special apparatus was required to allow men to escape from a sunken submarine. However, it was so bulky that it was impractical for the tiny submarines in service at the time.

COPING WITH RADIATION
The areas on board a submarine that contain nuclear material – the reactor compartment and the missile tubes – are built to the highest standards, remotely monitored, and designed to contain any initial mishap. If entry is required into those areas for investigative purposes, then special equipment is worn.

Radiation suit

The DSEA

THREAT FROM FIRE

Fire on board is probably the biggest danger in a modern submarine. Fire spreads quickly in such a cramped area, and it is very difficult for submariners to escape a burning vessel that is deep underwater. Although all submarines today carry breathing apparatus such as this oxygen mask, a fire on the Russian submarine *Komsoletts* in 1989 spread so badly out of control that it melted the hull and sank the submarine, drowning 42 of the crew.

Goggles

Nose-clip

Breathing hood

Oxygen mask to protect the wearer from poisonous gases.

Crewmen during a fire drill on the USS *Alabama*

FIRE DRILL

A well-trained submarine crew carries out fire drills and equipment checks at least once a week. Each crewmember learns how to wear an emergency breathing mask, and each has an agreed fire position. Some are trained to wear flame-resistant "fearnought" suits to enable them to tackle the cause of the fire.

Gloves to keep hands warm

Life jacket inflation bottle

Reflective patch to attract attention

ESCAPE SUIT

When HMS *Truculent* collided with a merchant ship on the Thames River in England in 1952 and was sunk, many of her crew managed to escape from the submarine. To everyone's horror , it was later found that many of those who escaped had died from drowning and extreme cold after they reached the surface. As a result, the escape suit was introduced. Not only does this provide protection against the cold, but it also protects the skin from fire and allows the survivor to float to the surface to be picked up by a rescue team.

Double-skinned feet to keep out the cold

ABANDON SHIP

This German-built submarine includes a separate escape section in which the crew can group together in an emergency. The section acts like an underwater lifeboat. It is detached from the hull and floated to the surface, where the crew can be rescued.

Pioneering the depths

Despite enormous progress over the years, crewed submarines can still reach only the upper regions of the ocean depths. To go deeper and cope with huge water pressures required the development of two vehicles. The first was the bathysphere—a large steel ball suspended on the end of a cable that could be lifted from a ship and lowered into the water. The second was the bathyscaphe—similar to the submarine, but with a massive flotation compartment and an observation ball underneath. With the arrival of the bathyscaphe, pioneers were finally able to reach the deepest point in the world.

THE FIRST DEEP–SEA EXPLORERS
In the 1920s, William Beebe and Otis Barton both explored their interest in nature. Together, the two Americans invented this steel bathysphere, which was lowered into the water with a cable. The first time that Beebe and Barton descended in their bathysphere off Bermuda in 1930, it leaked! With improvements, the bathysphere worked and went deeper than any other design at that time.

"Man lived with the stars, but the deep sea was beyond his ken."

AUGUSTE PICCARD

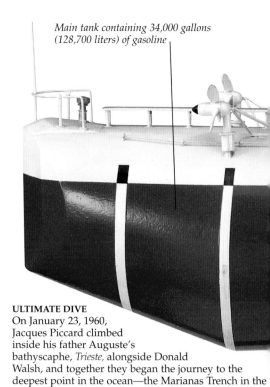

Main tank containing 34,000 gallons (128,700 liters) of gasoline

ULTIMATE DIVE
On January 23, 1960, Jacques Piccard climbed inside his father Auguste's bathyscaphe, *Trieste,* alongside Donald Walsh, and together they began the journey to the deepest point in the ocean—the Marianas Trench in the Pacific. Five hours later *Trieste* touched bottom at 37,730 ft (11,500 m). Built to resist pressures of up to 220,000 tons, the bathyscaphe was, and still is, the only craft to visit the lowest point on Earth.

UNDERWATER WORLD
By 1934, Beebe and Barton's steel bathysphere had set a world record when it reached a depth of 3,028 ft (920 m), taking 11 minutes to reach the end of the cable. Descending beneath the ocean surface, the two men explored the seabed and discovered deep-sea creatures that no one had seen before.

MASTER OF HEIGHT AND DEPTH

[Sw]iss-born Auguste Piccard took his hot-air [ba]lloon 10 miles (15 km) up in the sky in [after] realizing that gas in the inflated [would] expand as he went higher. In [1948], he turned this theory around [by] replacing gas with gasoline in his [bathy]scaphe *Trieste*. Iron ballast took [him] to the bottom of the ocean floor, [then] low-density aviation gasoline sent the craft back to the surface.

[C]ousteau's diving saucer, which made 123 dives

[P]ortholes for observation

[DI]VING SAUCER

[Al]though Beebe and Piccard broke [re]cords, it was Frenchman Jacques [C]ousteau who opened up the sea to the [w]orld. He designed and built diving [sa]ucers, like this 1959 model, that could [p]ower themselves along the sea floor. [Ev]entually, he created underwater work [st]ations where divers stayed for weeks.

Hole for observation

Carbon dioxide removers

Oxygen bottles

OBSERVATION CHAMBER

Later deep-sea craft became more advanced, as this example from 1930 shows. Still tethered to the surface, this one-man submersible observation chamber was designed to search shipwrecks before divers went down to take a look. The pilot inside would breathe air at normal pressure, and this was then recycled to remove carbon dioxide from the system.

TRIESTE

Ballast tank

Two-man observation sphere

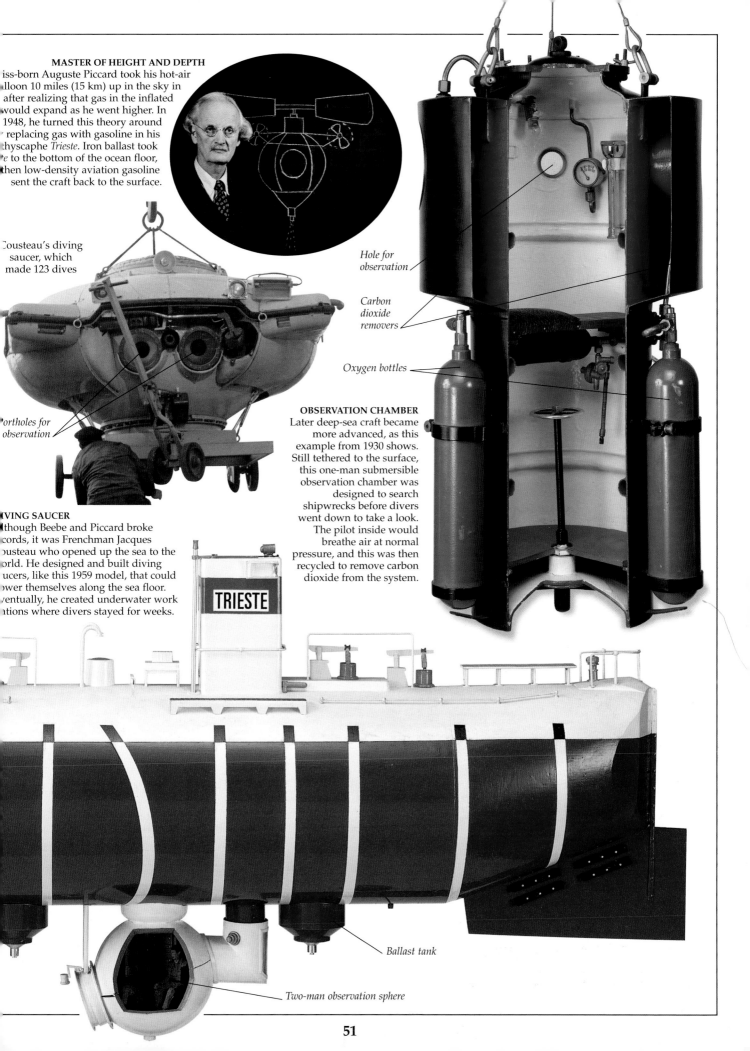

Into the abyss

SINCE WILLIAM BEEBE AND Auguste Piccard laid the foundations for deep-sea exploration in unconventional vessels, a whole new range of submersibles has arrived. Deep Research Vehicles (DRVs) and Remotely Operated Vehicles (ROVs) go much deeper than any modern submarine. Largely uncrewed, and produced by the hundreds, these exciting vehicles can also work in conditions beyond the capabilities of ordinary submarines. Many can be controlled by operators on the surface using closed-circuit television. Some can even be switched off and left on the sea floor between projects. These vehicles are exploring our seas as never before.

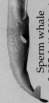

Holland I submarine 108 ft (33 m)

Scuba diver 475 ft (145 m)

SSN nuclear submarine 985 ft (300 m)

Armored diving suit 1,970 ft (600 m)

URN Deep Submergence rescue vehicle 2,460 ft (750 m)

Alfa deepest submarine 2,953 ft (900 m)

Beebe's bathysphere 3,280 ft (1,000 m)

Sperm whale 3,935 ft (1,200 m)

ROBOT HELPERS
ROVs such as robot helper *Argo* (above) assist with underwater missions. Built in 1982 for the US Navy, *Argo* is equipped with five video cameras and two sonar systems, and can be computer-controlled to "fly" at specified depths. Photographer Emory Kristof created the first designs for improving ROVs by adding electronic camera equipment. *Argo* was then updated and became the first craft to photograph the wreck of *Titanic* in 1985.

Support ship *Nadir* about to launch crewed *Nautile* to visit the wreck of *Titanic*

SUPPORT VESSELS
Although submersibles go to great depths, they are not designed for long-range travel on the surface. This is why modified support ships carry them to working locations. For uncrewed submersibles, the support ship is also the base where the underwater controls are operated.

52

Nautile
19,685 ft (6,000 m)

MIR
19,685 ft (6,000 m)

Shinkai submersible
21,325 ft (6,500 m)

Deepest fish
27,900 ft (8,500 m)

Trieste
37,730 ft (11,500 m)

SUPERSUBMARINE

The superstar of the submersible world is *Alvin*. This $1,000,000 craft entered service in 1964 and has completed over 3,000 dives. *Alvin's* underwater visits include locating an American H-bomb on the floor of the Mediterranean, discovering giant tubeworms in the Pacific Ocean, and visiting the wreck of *Titanic*. Once it was even attacked by a swordfish—trapped between *Alvin's* glass layers, the fish was taken to the surface and cooked for dinner!

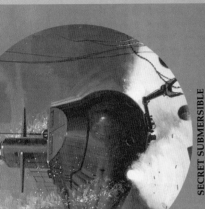

Alvin exploring the sea floor

SECRET SUBMERSIBLE

The US Navy's nuclear-powered *NR-1* was top-secret for many years, silently performing dozens of deep-sea missions. Still in use today, it was adapted to find lost wreckage and rarely resurfaces during an operation. When the space shuttle *Challenger* crashed in 1986, *NR-1* found the scattered remains. Here, *NR-1* extends its "claw" to lift the wreck of a crashed Navy jet.

Shinkai 6500

DEEPEST OF ALL

Most commercial submersibles are built to withstand pressures down to 10,000 ft (300 m) below the surface. Only a few can go below this depth. However, *Shinkai 6500* is a Japanese crewed research submersible that can dive to 21,325 ft, or 6,500 m, as its name suggests. Completed in 1990, *Shinkai 6500* plays an important part in deep-sea research and earthquake prediction.

Shipwreck

UNTIL THE ARRIVAL OF deep-sea exploration vehicles, the majority of shipwrecks remained unseen and untouched, except for the occasional shallow-water discovery. Now that it is possible to identify and visit the wrecks of maritime disasters, ships such as *Titanic*, *Bismarck*, and *Hood* have become key sites of exploration for historians. Wreck visits will increase at all depths as the fascination surrounding these disasters continues. But historians bringing artifacts to the surface are often accused of "treasure-hunting" and "tomb-raiding." People question whether it is right to disturb the resting place of so many sailors and passengers.

DEEPEST DEPTHS
Early theory maintained that ships did not fall to the bottom of the oceans, but remained suspended in a mid-pressure area. Underwater exploration showed that this was a myth when wrecks were discovered in the depths. Wrecks lying many miles down in the deepest seas have so far eluded all efforts to find them. The condition of shipwrecks at these depths will be a source of interest to historians.

WRECK LOCATOR
In 1773, the huge British ship *The Royal Captain*, carrying 100,000 pieces of valuable Chinese porcelain, sank in the South China Sea. It took two centuries and a crewed submersible to locate the wreck and recover part of the cargo. Frenchman Franck Goddio calculated the possible location of the disaster before making his discovery. He is seen here with a pilot, labeling the rotting timbers of *The Royal Captain* with special foam number tags designed to resist water pressure and stay in position. The submersible is bubble-shaped to view the outstanding features of a shipwreck.

EXPLORER OF THE DEEP
Perhaps the greatest living underwater historian is Rober Ballard (US), seen here with a model of *Bismarck*. Using remote-control vehicles, he has located and explored a number of famous wrecks, including *Titanic*.

Controllers using robotic arms to mark out the remains of the shipwreck.

296

BROUGHT TO THE SURFACE
Launched in 1985, the French-built *Nautile* is a crewed exploration submersible. It is famous for a dive in 1989 during which geologists in the vehicle collected samples that revealed how forces shape Earth's crust. The submersible has also investigated wrecks, including that of *Titanic*.

ON THE SURFACE
While wreck investigation is regarded as historical research, taking artifacts from sunken ships is controversial. *Titanic* hit an iceberg and sank on its maiden voyage in 1912, killing more than 1,500 people. By 1987, *Nautile* had made 32 dives to the ruins of *Titanic*, taking a variety of objects.

Titanic's cherub from the Grand Staircase

The remains of a letter that sank with *Titanic*

Playing cards from *Titanic*

Plaque lies on wreck of *Bismarck*

WATERY GRAVE
In 1941, the British and German navies clashed in the Atlantic. Battle Cruiser *Hood* blew up and sank, followed by *Bismarck*—on her first operational cruise. Warships such as these usually carry the protection of being classed as war graves, which cannot be visited. Robert Ballard found both ships and placed commemorative war plaques on the wreckage.

Bismarck war plaque

Japanese mini-sub

SUB FINDS SUB
The surprise attack by the Japanese Air Force on Pearl Harbor, Hawaii on December 7, 1941, is well documented. Less well known is that several Japanese midget submarines provided information in advance for the aircraft—five midgets were sunk in the process. This Type A Japanese midget was discovered in 2002 by the crewed Hawaii Undersea Research Laboratory.

Creatures of the deep

Sɪɴᴄᴇ ᴛʜᴇ 1950s, the rapid development of research submersibles has led to the discovery of an astonishing variety of deep-sea life. Expeditions have found all kinds of animals that are able to live in conditions where humans could not possibly survive. In this mysterious world of almost total darkness, extreme cold, and tremendous pressure, fish and other animals need special adaptations to survive. Food is scarce, and so are breeding partners. Many deep-sea fish are able to generate their own light to lure prey and to attract partners. Every year, new species of fish are identified at massive depths, but this is only a drop in the ocean compared to what is left to explore.

SPECIMEN COLLECTIC
In the 1870s, the ship F *Challenger* dredged the oceans to collect 13,00(plants and animals, su this lobster. Today, ma submersibles can colle even delicate creatures special containers built withstand the immense pressures at great dept

Dana viperfish

THE DEEP-SEA ZOO
Living at depths of 3,000 ft (900 m) or more, these fish have many adaptations to the deep-sea environment. Their huge eyes can detect the faintest glimmer of light. Their soft, flexible skeletons are not crushed by the pressure of all the water pressing down on them from above. These fish also have gaping jaws, sharp teeth, and stretchy stomachs that enable them to take full advantage of any food they are lucky enough to find.

Hatchetfish

Fish develops inside egg sac.

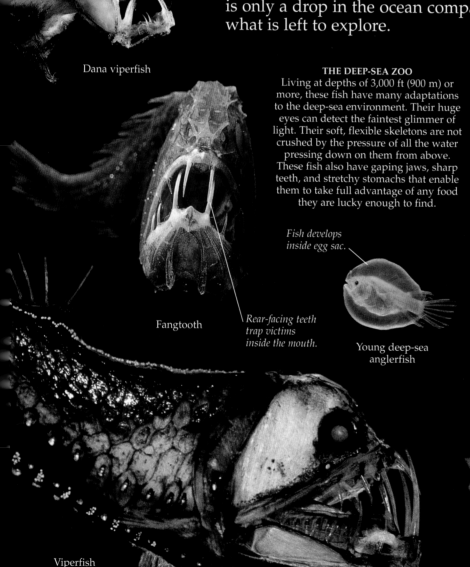

Fangtooth

Rear-facing teeth trap victims inside the mouth.

Young deep-sea anglerfish

Viperfish

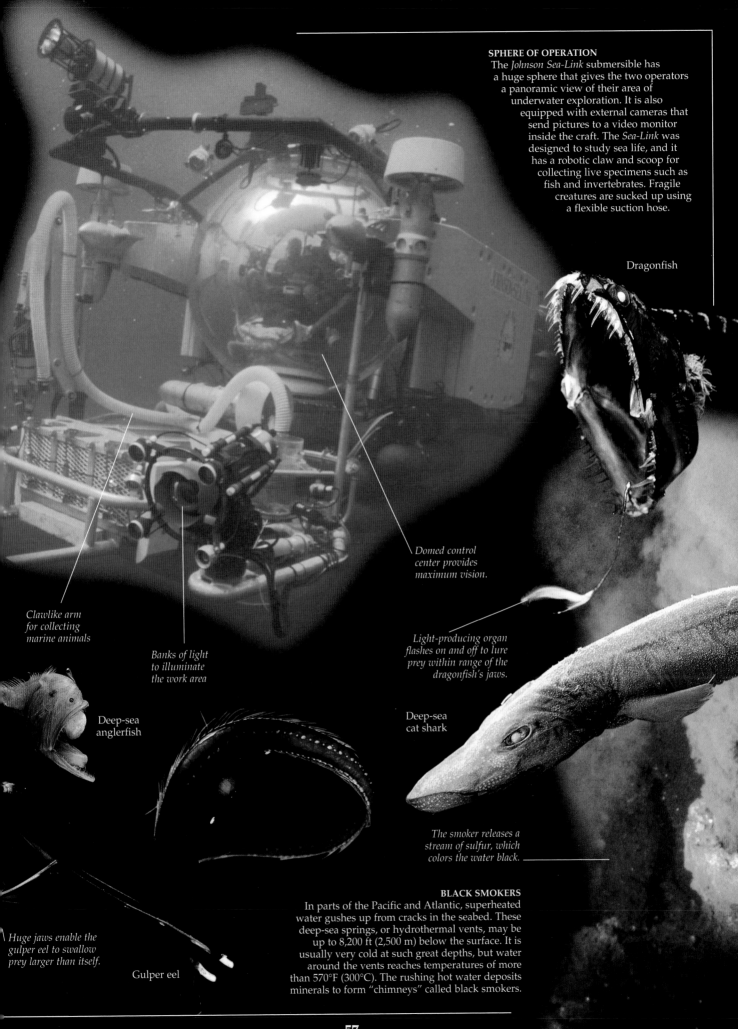

The *Johnson Sea-Link* submersible has a huge sphere that gives the two operators a panoramic view of their area of underwater exploration. It is also equipped with external cameras that send pictures to a video monitor inside the craft. The *Sea-Link* was designed to study sea life, and it has a robotic claw and scoop for collecting live specimens such as fish and invertebrates. Fragile creatures are sucked up using a flexible suction hose.

Dragonfish

Domed control center provides maximum vision.

Clawlike arm for collecting marine animals

Banks of light to illuminate the work area

Light-producing organ flashes on and off to lure prey within range of the dragonfish's jaws.

Deep-sea anglerfish

Deep-sea cat shark

The smoker releases a stream of sulfur, which colors the water black.

BLACK SMOKERS
In parts of the Pacific and Atlantic, superheated water gushes up from cracks in the seabed. These deep-sea springs, or hydrothermal vents, may be up to 8,200 ft (2,500 m) below the surface. It is usually very cold at such great depths, but water around the vents reaches temperatures of more than 570°F (300°C). The rushing hot water deposits minerals to form "chimneys" called black smokers.

Huge jaws enable the gulper eel to swallow prey larger than itself.

Gulper eel

Workers beneath the waves

JUST LIKE SOME SATELLITES and spacecraft, commercial submersibles are controlled and monitored from a central base. Television pictures and other data help operators to follow the progress of the underwater craft from the surface. They can make the Remotely Operated Vehicles (ROVs) hover, move quickly, or land. Various parts of the vehicle can be controlled, including cameras, claws, and sample-takers. Larger vehicles can sink to 10,000 ft (3,050 m), while some mini-robots are small enough to fit inside pipelines. Although ROVs are expensive to run, they have many advantages. They can explore murky depths, carry out vital repairs to oil rigs, and investigate shipwrecks without risking human life.

PIPE INSPECTION
The ultimate ROV is the pipe inspection camera. Seen here about to be launched from the surface, the camera is designed to fit inside an underwater pipeline. The water-flow through the pipe propels the camera along as it records video pictures of the pipe's condition.

Good visibility for the operator

Springy arms assist movement underwater, while "claws" can grip and manipulate objects.

Thruster provides power

WASP SUIT
The one-man "Wasp" is a diving suit that can work at depths of up to 2,000 ft (610 m). The pilot pictured here is Graham Hawkes. He uses the viewing bubble to inspect the oil fields, and the robotic manipulator arms to complete any difficult jobs. The suit bounces along the bottom, powered by thrusters around the middle. The wearer operates these with foot pedals.

OIL RIG SAFETY
An oil rig hides a lot more under the sea than is seen on the surface. Many oil rigs far offshore have their own ROVs to make regular checks on their underwater structure. These ROVs check that the supporting legs of the rig are standing firm, and warn of any faults that may need repairing. The ROVs also look at the oil pipelines running over the sea-bed to make sure they are safe.

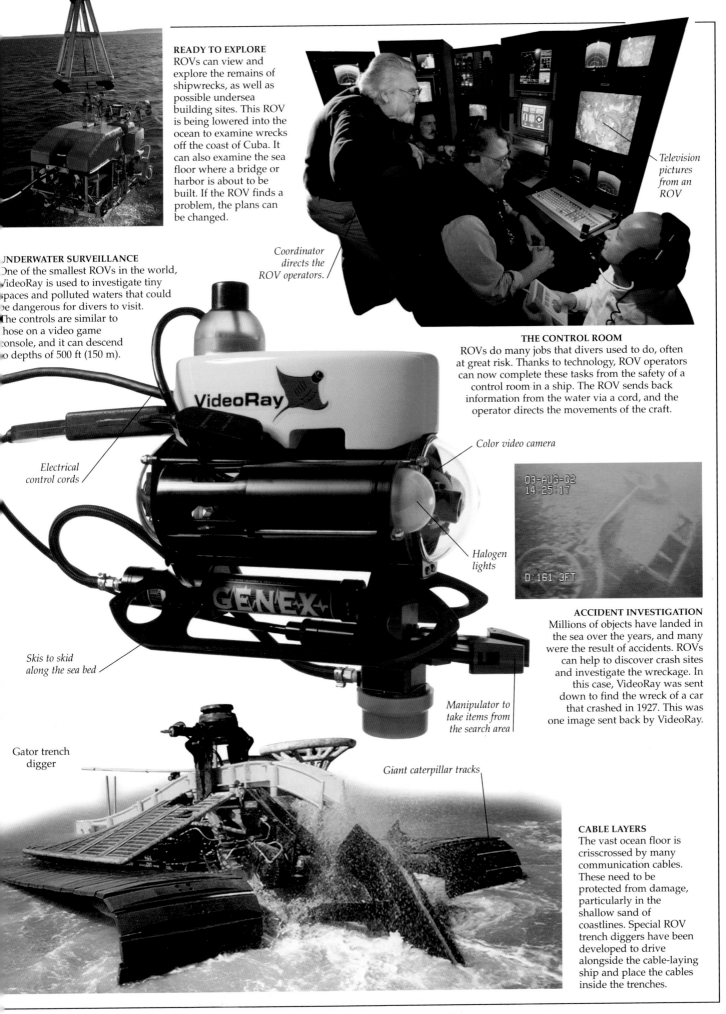

READY TO EXPLORE
ROVs can view and explore the remains of shipwrecks, as well as possible undersea building sites. This ROV is being lowered into the ocean to examine wrecks off the coast of Cuba. It can also examine the sea floor where a bridge or harbor is about to be built. If the ROV finds a problem, the plans can be changed.

Television pictures from an ROV

Coordinator directs the ROV operators.

UNDERWATER SURVEILLANCE
One of the smallest ROVs in the world, VideoRay is used to investigate tiny spaces and polluted waters that could be dangerous for divers to visit. The controls are similar to those on a video game console, and it can descend to depths of 500 ft (150 m).

THE CONTROL ROOM
ROVs do many jobs that divers used to do, often at great risk. Thanks to technology, ROV operators can now complete these tasks from the safety of a control room in a ship. The ROV sends back information from the water via a cord, and the operator directs the movements of the craft.

Electrical control cords

Color video camera

Halogen lights

03-AUG-02
14:25:17
D:161.3FT

ACCIDENT INVESTIGATION
Millions of objects have landed in the sea over the years, and many were the result of accidents. ROVs can help to discover crash sites and investigate the wreckage. In this case, VideoRay was sent down to find the wreck of a car that crashed in 1927. This was one image sent back by VideoRay.

Skis to skid along the sea bed

Manipulator to take items from the search area

Gator trench digger

Giant caterpillar tracks

CABLE LAYERS
The vast ocean floor is crisscrossed by many communication cables. These need to be protected from damage, particularly in the shallow sand of coastlines. Special ROV trench diggers have been developed to drive alongside the cable-laying ship and place the cables inside the trenches.

Subs for fun

DESPITE THEIR INVOLVEMENT IN war, submarines became a form of entertainment in the second half of the 20th century. The public was fascinated with these exciting machines, and businesses realized that they could make money out of fun submarines. Lake's idea of a submarine on wheels (p. 20) finally became a reality at Disneyland, where model submarines running on rails took visitors around the park. In the 1960s, world-famous band The Beatles made a cartoon film about a yellow submarine. Submarines began to carry tourists, and luxury submarines were built. Now there are even submarine museums and underwater hotels.

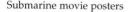

Submarine movie posters

SUBMARINE MOVIES

Submarine films came to life after World War II when they had much more history to base the action on. In particular, German-produced *Das Boot* (1981) showed the reality of being on a U-boat. Later, *The Hunt for Red October* (1990) provided a look at a nuclear submarine involved in war. Famous fictional characters such as James Bond have had adventures on board submarines, while The Beatles' *Yellow Submarine* (1968) and Disney's *Atlantis* (2001) each included a colorful and action-packed submarine in their stories.

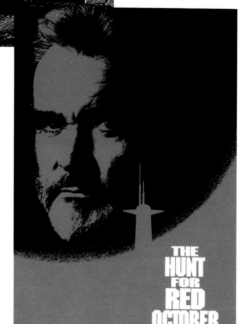

SUBMARINE MUSEUM

Submarines such as USS *Bowfin* have been turned into popular museums. Built in 1943, USS *Bowfin* has long since stopped working, but is still in Hawaii, where it was based at Pearl Harbor. Visitors can walk around and experience the boat as it was when it was in service. However, a clean submarine, without the engine smell and constant noise, would be a strange place to a crewman who had served on USS *Bowfin*.

Cramped crew quarters on USS *Bowfin*

A LIFE OF LUXURY

If you have $78 million to spare, this personal submarine could be yours. *Phoenix 1000* is the world's first luxury submarine. It runs on the surface with diesel engines, dives on battery power, and resurfaces to recharge the batteries. It is possible to stay submerged for days. Designed to be as comfortable and safe as possible, personal submarines dive to about 1,000 ft (300 m).

Control planes

Propulsion motor

SUBMARINE RIDE

In the 1980s, the safest submarines in the world were to be found in Disneyland, California. The theme park ride allowed passengers to ride in the hull below the water and look out of the portholes. For safety reasons, the submarines never actually dived. As with many pleasure submarines, they were all yellow, like the one in the Beatles' movie.

Viewing area for passengers

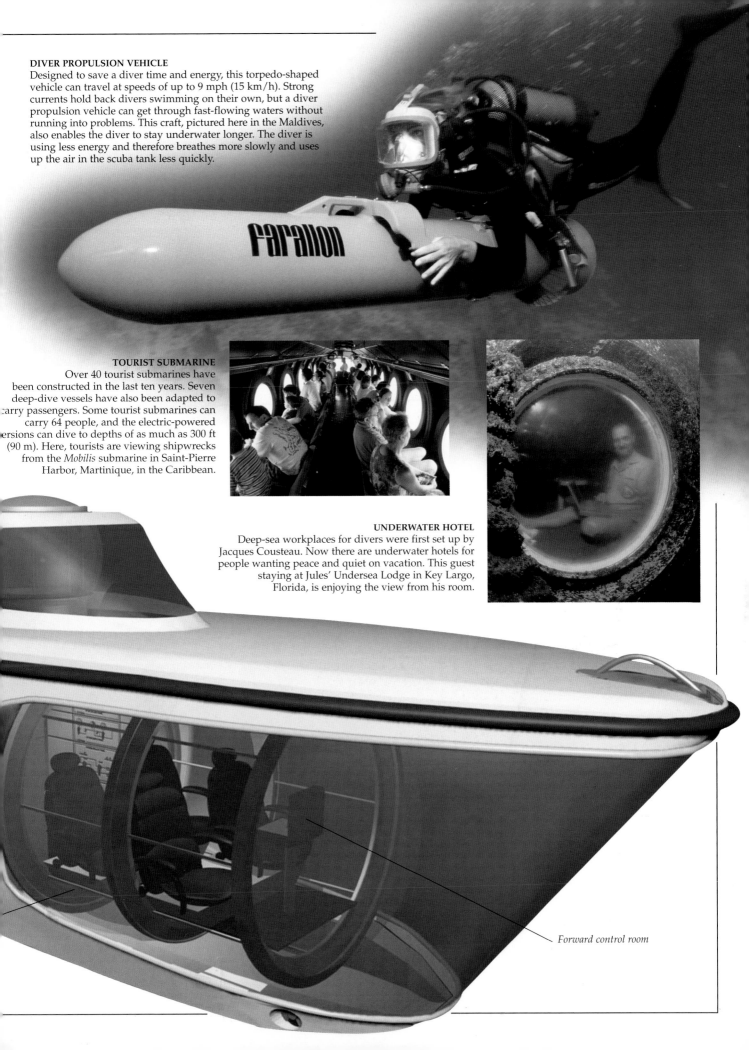

DIVER PROPULSION VEHICLE
Designed to save a diver time and energy, this torpedo-shaped vehicle can travel at speeds of up to 9 mph (15 km/h). Strong currents hold back divers swimming on their own, but a diver propulsion vehicle can get through fast-flowing waters without running into problems. This craft, pictured here in the Maldives, also enables the diver to stay underwater longer. The diver is using less energy and therefore breathes more slowly and uses up the air in the scuba tank less quickly.

TOURIST SUBMARINE
Over 40 tourist submarines have been constructed in the last ten years. Seven deep-dive vessels have also been adapted to carry passengers. Some tourist submarines can carry 64 people, and the electric-powered versions can dive to depths of as much as 300 ft (90 m). Here, tourists are viewing shipwrecks from the *Mobilis* submarine in Saint-Pierre Harbor, Martinique, in the Caribbean.

UNDERWATER HOTEL
Deep-sea workplaces for divers were first set up by Jacques Cousteau. Now there are underwater hotels for people wanting peace and quiet on vacation. This guest staying at Jules' Undersea Lodge in Key Largo, Florida, is enjoying the view from his room.

Forward control room

Subs of the future

VISIONS OF THE FUTURE
The Victorians imagined using the submarine as underwater transportation, following various routes, with one early proposal to shuttle passengers across the English Channel. In fact, many of their 19th-century dreams and ideas have now become reality, as science catches up with concepts.

THE SUBMARINE WILL CONTINUE to play an important role in the 21st century. Wealthy nations will build and maintain nuclear submarines, while others update their standard diesel-electric versions. A top priority for engineers and designers will be to develop new methods of powering submarines. More deep-sea exploration will take place as more artifacts and minerals are brought to the surface. From the tiny "submarine" that could soon be visiting the inside of the human body, to large research submarines that may head out to explore the seas of other worlds, the range of tasks for submarines to tackle will be wider than ever before.

Movable jet thrusters replace the old-style propeller.

Streamlined hull

STATE-OF-THE-ART
This is a possible military submarine of the future, designed by British Aerospace. The nose contains an array of sensors, the smooth hull is made from new high-tech materials, and the craft drives through the water with movable jet thrusters. This state-of-the-art craft will carry a group of underwater vehicles to search for targets and defend the submarine.

Storage for underwater robots

"Knowledge of the oceans is more than a matter of curiosity. Our very survival may hinge upon it."

PRESIDENT JOHN F. KENNEDY
Message to Congress, March 1961

SUBMARINES IN SPACE
This is an artist's impression of a future NASA mission involving a submarine on one of the moons of the planet Jupiter. Scientists want to investigate whether there is an ocean under the surface of Europa. They plan to explore the surface layer using a remotely controlled submarine called a hydrobot. If this is successful, a hydrobot will be used to explore other solar-system bodies with large areas of water.

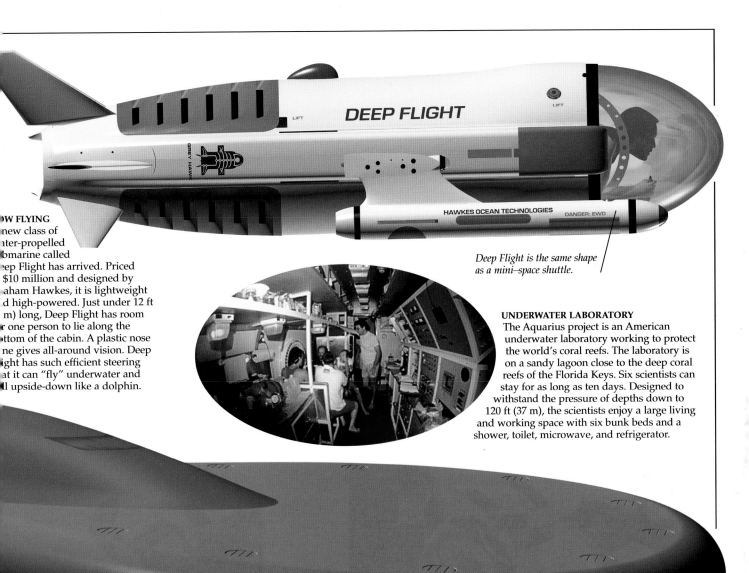

DEEP FLIGHT

HAWKES OCEAN TECHNOLOGIES   DANGER: EWO

Deep Flight is the same shape as a mini–space shuttle.

[FL]OW FLYING
[A] new class of
[wa]ter-propelled
[su]bmarine called
[De]ep Flight has arrived. Priced
[at $]10 million and designed by
[Gr]aham Hawkes, it is lightweight
[an]d high-powered. Just under 12 ft
[(4 m) long, Deep Flight has room
[fo]r one person to lie along the
[bo]ttom of the cabin. A plastic nose
[co]ne gives all-around vision. Deep
[Fl]ight has such efficient steering
[th]at it can "fly" underwater and
[rol]l upside-down like a dolphin.

UNDERWATER LABORATORY
The Aquarius project is an American
underwater laboratory working to protect
the world's coral reefs. The laboratory is
on a sandy lagoon close to the deep coral
reefs of the Florida Keys. Six scientists can
stay for as long as ten days. Designed to
withstand the pressure of depths down to
120 ft (37 m), the scientists enjoy a large living
and working space with six bunk beds and a
shower, toilet, microwave, and refrigerator.

[M]ODULAR TECHNOLOGY
[T]he modern Virginia-Class nuclear
[su]bmarine has a variety of sections that
[c]an be lifted out, modified, or replaced
[ac]cording to the needs of the vessel. Future
[su]bmarines may be adapted like this so that
[n]ew technologies can easily be added.

FANTASTIC VOYAGE
The next step in medical technology will be investigations by a tiny submarine. In 1966,
science-fiction writer Isaac Asimov drew the nanoscale submarine shown here and called it
"Fantastic Voyage." The hope is that one day the nanoscale submarine will be able to move
through the human bloodstream, destroying diseased cells on the way.

Index

Acknowledgments

Dorling Kindersley would like to thank: Leah Germann, Steve Savage, Ben Hoare, Jo Connor.

The publishers would like to thank the following for their kind permission to reproduce their photographs:
a=above; b=below; c=center; l=left; r=right; t=top
Art Directors & Eyewitness Submarine Picture Credits
Agence France Presse: 30crb; AKG London: 18tl, 18-19; British Library 12tr; U-Boat U53 Sinking a British Steamer by Claus Friedrich Bergen © DACS 2003 18tr; Bovington Tank Museum: 2l; Tim Brown: 9cra, 15t, 22-23, 28-29, 28-29, 29cra, 29cr, 39tr, 43b, 44cbl, 52tcl, 52tcr, 52tcrr, 62-63; Corbis: 23tr, 25tr, 38cl, 42b; Bettmann 22tl, 27cr, 28c, 47crb, 50tr, 51tc, 51cla, 56tl; Jonathan Blair 59tr; Horace Bristol 41tl; Philip James Corwin 60bc; Bob Duff 41r;

Stephen Frink 61cr; JO1 Joe Gawlowicz 41cl; General Dynamics Electric Boat Division 11br; Philip Gould 61ca; George Hall 43tr; Hulton-Deutsch Collection 10bc, 35tl, 47c; WO Jack January 22-23; Steve Kaufman 30l, 31tl, 33b, 36bc, 40br; Larry Lee Photography 58crb; The Mariners' Museum 19tr, 42cla; Joe Marquette / Bettmann 54cra; Chris McLaughlin 57tc; PH1 Robert McRoy 41tl; PHC(DV) Mark Reinhard 6-7; Roger Ressmeyer 7bc, 36cl, 36-37, 49tl; Paul A. Sounders 59tl; Stocktrek 26l; Peter Turnley 29br; United States Navy 26-27; Ralph White 7tr, 52cl, 52cr, 53bl, 53tcl, 55tr; Yogi, Inc. 31tr, 39b; Department of National Defence/ Canadian Forces: 37tc; Mary Evans Picture Library: 13tr, 16tr, 50bl, 54tl, 62tl; Eyevine Ltd: Corona Films / Zed / Saola 37c, 37br, 48br; Global Marine Systems Limited: From the archives of Global Marine Systems Limited 59b; Frank Goddio: Hilti Foundation / Christoph Gerigk 54-55b; Ronald Grant

Archive: Paramount Pictures 60cal; Hawkes Ocean Technologies/ www.deepflight.com: 63t; Ric Hedman TN(SS): 20cl; Imperial War Museum: 18cl, 42cra; Itar-tass Photo Agency: Semyon Maisterman 46-47; JAMSTEC: 53c; Kobal Collection: Bavaria/Radiant 60tl; David L. Mearns / Blue Water Recoveries Ltd: 55c, 55cr; NASA: 62bl; The Natural History Museum, London: 56tr; Naval Historical Foundation: 20tr; N.H.P.A.: Ernie Janes 48car; Norbert Wu 53tcr, 56cl, 56cb, 56bl, 56br, 57cr, 57clb, 57crb, 57bl; NOAA: Courtesy of NOAA's Undersea Research Center at the University of North Carolina at Wilmington 63ca; Hawaii Undersea Research Laboratory, University of Hawaii 55br; OAR/Nationalk Undersea Research Program; JAMSTEC 53tc; R. Wicklund/OAR/National Undersea Research Program (NURP) 58bl; Novosti (London): 27cl; Oxford Scientific Films: Paulo De Oliveira 56cla; Popperfoto: 6bl, 12crb; Reuters 41ca; Rex Features: Nils Jorgensen 55tl, 55cl, 55cbl; The Royal Navy Submarine Museum: 6tr, 8-9, 9cl, 9crb, 10cl, 11cr, 12c, 12-13, 13tl, 13cl, 15tr, 15cl, 15br, 16cb, 17cl, 17c,

17t, 19cl, 21cr, 21t, 23crb, 24c, 24b, 25clb, 26ca, 28cal, 28l, 31br, 32tl, 34tl, 34cr, 34crb, 38tr, 40tl, 40c, 41clb, 41bc, 43tl, 44tl, 44cl, 45c, 46tl, 46bl, 47tr, 47br, 48cl, 48cr, 49bl, 49r, 52tl; Royal Tropical Institute: 52tc; Science Photo Library: ESA / CE / Eurocontrol 45tc; W. Haxby, Lamont-Doherty Earth Observatory 45bc; Coneyl Jay 63br; Dr. Ken Macdonald 45bcl; B. Murton/ Southampton Oceanography Centre 57br; Alexis Rosenfeld 7cr, 61tr; F.S. Westmorland 52-53; TRH Pictures: 19tl; Associated Press 24ca; Courtesy of U.S. Air Force: 28bl; Courtesy of US Navy: John E. Gay 44-45; US Navy Submarine Force Museum, Groton: 14bl, 22bl, 25ca, 25br, 53cla; U.S. Submarines Inc.: 60-61; VideoRay LLC: With permission of VideoRay LLC - www.videoray.com 59c, 59cr.

All other images © Dorling Kindersley
For further information see:
www.dkimages.com